CHRIST

HISTORY

RESURRECTION

INCARNATION

SANTA CLAUS

TRADITIONS

MIRACLES

ADVENT

SALVATION

Published in Nashville, Tennessee, by Thomas Nelson. Thomas Nelson is a registered trademark of Thomas Nelson, Inc.

Thomas Nelson, Inc., titles may be purchased in bulk for educational, business, fund-raising, or sales promotional use. For information, please e-mail SpecialMarkets@ThomasNelson.com.

All Scriptures are from the HOLY BIBLE: NEW INTERNATIONAL VERSION®. © 1973, 1978, 1984 by International Bible Society. Used by permission of Zondervan Publishing House. All rights reserved.

ISBN-13: 978-1-4041-8758-0

Printed in the United States of America
09 10 11 12 13 [HH] 6 5 4 3 2

www.equip.org
www.thomasnelson.com

THE
HEART
OF

Christmas

> A Devotional for the Season

HANK HANEGRAAFF

THOMAS NELSON
Since 1798

NASHVILLE   DALLAS   MEXICO CITY   RIO DE JANEIRO   BEIJING

INTRODUCTION

Each year during Christmas, I communicate the truth concerning Christ's coming in flesh. This year I want to take the *truths* of Christmas and turn them into a Christmas *tradition*. As such, the purpose of *The Heart of Christmas: A Devotional for the Season* is to ensure that just as you prepare your home for Christmas, you will likewise prepare your heart.

As the culture begins promoting Christmas shopping the day after Thanksgiving, Christians can begin preparing their hearts for the celebration of Jesus' birth. It is my hope and prayer that this year you will use this devotional for the season to begin a Christmas tradition that carries on until the year in which you meet your Savior face-to-face—and that even in your absence, your loved ones will carry the tradition forward.

To make the journey memorable, I've organized this twenty-five-day odyssey around the acronym C-H-R-I-S-T-M-A-S.

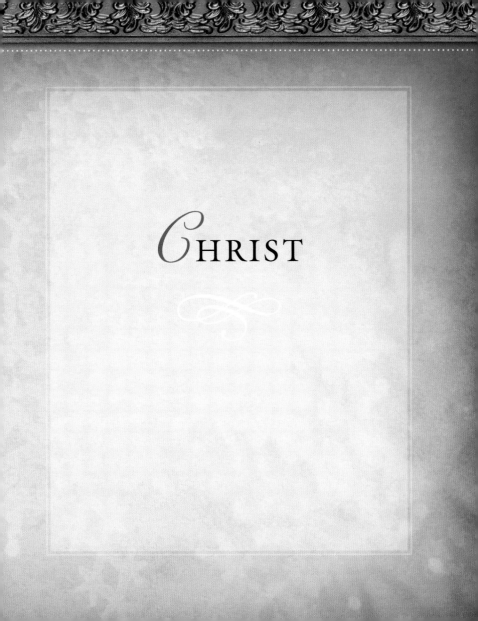

CHRIST

THE LONG-AWAITED CHRIST

Today in the town of David a Savior has been born to you;
he is Christ the Lord.

—LUKE 2:11

W e begin our journey to the heart of Christmas by zeroing in on the word *Christ*. In a biblically illiterate culture, many mistakenly suppose that *Christ* represents the last name of Jesus. In truth, *Christ* is a title that comes from the Greek (*Christos*) rendering of the Hebrew word *Messiah*, meaning "anointed one." As such, the Christ of Christmas is the long-awaited Messiah who fulfills all the types and shadows of the Old Testament Scriptures.

To fully grasp the significance of Christ's messianic role, you must drink deeply from the wellspring of Old Testament prophecy. In Hebrews, as in the rest of the New Testament, the Old Testament history of Israel is interpreted as a succession of types that find ultimate fulfillment in the birth, death, resurrection, and ascension of the Christ we celebrate at Christmas.

In his letter to the Romans, Paul refers to Adam as a "pattern" (literally, *type*) of Jesus Christ (Romans 5:14). Likewise, Paul taught the believers at Colosse that the dietary laws, religious festivals, and Sabbath of the Old Covenant were "a shadow of the things that were to come; the reality, however, is found in Christ" (Colossians 2:17).

The interpretive principle of typology is equally persuasive in the Gospels. Christ's successful resistance of temptation in the desert after forty days of fasting is a direct typological contrast to the disobedience of the Israelites that resulted in forty years of wilderness wanderings (Matthew 4:1-11; Mark 1:12-13; Luke 4:1-13). In remaining faithful to His Father, Christ did what Israel was unable to do. Christ is thus the true Israel, and all who are found in Christ are heirs according to the promises God made to Abraham (Galatians 3:29).

Moreover, Jesus is revealed as the *antitype* (that to which the type points) of the Hebrew prophets through His preaching of repentance, His ministry of healing, His concern for the poor and social outcasts, and His death near Jerusalem. Though like the prophets in these ways, Christ is shown to be greater than all the previous prophets in the manner of His miraculous ministry, His claims to be God, and the vindication of those claims in His resurrection. According to Luke's gospel, Jesus Himself, "beginning with Moses and all the Prophets . . . explained to [his disciples] what was said in all the Scriptures concerning himself" (Luke 24:27).

Today as you ponder the Christ of Christmas, remember that it is He alone who could emerge through the doorway of the Old Testament Scriptures.

→ ———————————— READING ———————————— ←

Today in the town of David a Savior has been born to you; he is Christ the Lord. This will be a sign to you: You will find a baby wrapped in cloths and lying in a manger.

Suddenly a great company of the heavenly host appeared with the angel, praising God and saying,

"Glory to God in the highest, and on earth peace to men on whom his favor rests." (Luke 2:11–14)

→ ———————————— QUESTIONS ———————————— ←

+ What is the meaning of the word *Christ*?
+ What are some of the Old Testament types and shadows that find fulfillment in Christ?

JOY TO THE WORLD
Isaac Watts

Joy to the world, the Lord is come!
Let earth receive her King;

Let every heart prepare Him room,
And heaven and nature sing,
And heaven and nature sing,
And heaven, and heaven, and nature sing.

Joy to the earth, the Savior reigns!
Let men their songs employ;
While fields and floods,
Rocks, hills and plains
Repeat the sounding joy,
Repeat the sounding joy,
Repeat, repeat, the sounding joy.

No more let sins and sorrows grow,
Nor thorns infest the ground;
He comes to make His blessing flow
Far as the curse is found,

Far as the curse is found,
Far as, far as, the curse is found.

He rules the world with truth and grace,
And makes the nations prove
The glories of His righteousness,
And wonders of His love,
And wonders of His love,
And wonders, wonders, of His love.

Day 2

ISAIAH'S PROPHECY

*All this took place to fulfill what the Lord had said through the prophet:
"The virgin will be with child and will give birth to a son, and they will
call him Immanuel"—which means, "God with us."*

—MATTHEW 1:22–23

H ave you ever stopped for just a moment to ponder the majesty of the word *Immanuel*? It is incredible to consider that when Isaiah, the holiest man in Israel, prophesied, "The virgin will be with child and will give birth to a son, and they will call him Immanuel," he was literally predicting that in the future the One who spoke the limitless galaxies into existence would tabernacle in flesh among men. Indeed, that is precisely what the word *Immanuel* means—"God with us."

As we continue our journey toward Christmas Day, let's take just a moment to consider the context of perhaps the best-known of all Old Testament prophecies. In context, Isaiah foresees impending doom looming on the horizon. But he also foresees a coming Messiah who would ultimately deliver God's people from their sins.

The near-future fulfillment of Isaiah's prophecy (Isaiah 8) confirmed to his contemporaries that he was indeed a true prophet of God. While the Holy Spirit may have revealed another layer of meaning as a far-future messianic prophecy, the foremost concern of Isaiah and his contemporaries was the protection of Judah against her enemies. Indeed, Judah was "shaken" as two powerful kingdoms sought her demise (see 7:1–2). God, however, promised King Ahaz that the birth of Isaiah's son Maher-Shalal-Hash-Baz would be a sign that Judah would be spared. In the words of Isaiah, "Before the boy knows enough to reject the wrong and choose the right, the land of the two kings you dread will be laid waste" (7:16; cf. 8:4). It should be noted that while Isaiah's wife (unlike Mary) was not a virgin when she gave birth to Maher-Shalal-Hash-Baz, she was nonetheless the fore-future fulfillment of Isaiah's prophecy. *Virgin* (*almah*) was simply a term used to refer to the prophetess prior to her union with Isaiah—not that she would give birth to a child *as* a virgin.

It was not until after the birth of Jesus seven hundred years later that it became entirely clear that the near-future fulfillment of Isaiah's prophecy in the birth of his son Maher-Shalal-Hash-Baz was a type, the antitype of which was Jesus the Messiah (Matthew 1:22–23). While Maher-Shalal-Hash-Baz was a sign guaranteeing God's temporal salvation of Judah, Jesus Christ—the true Immanuel—not only signified but embodied the ultimate and eternal salvation of God's chosen ones from sin and death.

→ ——————— READING ——————— ←

The Lord himself will give you a sign: The virgin will be with child and will give birth to a son, and will call him Immanuel. (Isaiah 7:14)

→ ——————— QUESTIONS ——————— ←

+ What are similarities and differences between the births of Maher-Shalal-Hash-Baz and Jesus Christ?
+ Some say that Matthew misunderstood Isaiah's Immanuel prophecy, because the prediction in chapter 7 of Isaiah is fulfilled in chapter 8. How does Matthew's understanding of typology solve the problem?

O Come All Ye Faithful

Traditional Carol

O come, all ye faithful, joyful and triumphant,
O come ye, O come ye, to Bethlehem.
Come and behold Him, born the King of angels;
O come, let us adore Him,
O come, let us adore Him,
O come, let us adore Him,
Christ the Lord.

God of God, Light of Light,
Lo, He abhors not the Virgin's womb,
Very God, begotten, not created;
O come, let us adore Him,
O come, let us adore Him,
O come, let us adore Him,
Christ the Lord.

Sing, choirs of angels, sing in exultation;
Sing, all ye citizens of heaven above!
Glory to God, in the highest;
O come, let us adore Him,

O come, let us adore Him,
O come, let us adore Him,
Christ the Lord.

Yea, Lord, we greet Thee, born this happy morning;
Jesus, to Thee be glory given;
Word of the Father, now in flesh appearing.
O come, let us adore Him,
O come, let us adore Him,
O come, let us adore Him,
Christ the Lord.

THE GOLDEN KEY OF MESSIANIC PROPHECIES

*And beginning with Moses and all the Prophets, he [Jesus] explained
to them what was said in all the Scriptures concerning himself.*

—LUKE 24:27

Prophecy represents one of the most powerful proofs of the divine origins of the biblical text. The book of Daniel is a classic case in point. In the midst of the sixth-century-BC Babylonian captivity, YHWH reveals, through Daniel, His present and eternal purposes for Israel and the world. Daniel accurately predicts the progression of kingdoms from Babylon through the Median and Persian empires to the further persecution and suffering of the Jews under Antiochus IV Epiphanes, including the Syrian despot's desecration of the Jerusalem Temple, his untimely death, and freedom for the Jews under Judas Maccabeus in 165 BC.

Moreover, the book of Daniel prophetically looks forward to the coming of Messiah. As prophesied by Jeremiah, Jerusalem would experience a partial restoration after seventy years of exile (Jeremiah 29:10); however, as revealed through the angel Gabriel, the return from exile was merely a type of the antitypical freedom that would be experienced through Judas Maccabeus, which itself was typological of ultimate restoration through Jesus the Messiah.

Since Christ is the fulfillment of the law and the prophets, it should not surprise us that prophecies regarding Him outnumber all others. Many of these prophecies would have been impossible for Jesus to deliberately conspire to fulfill—such as His descent from Abraham, Isaac, and Jacob (Genesis 12:3; 17:19); His birth in Bethlehem (Micah 5:2); His crucifixion with criminals (Isaiah 53:12); the piercing of His hands and feet on the cross (Psalm 22:16); the soldiers' gambling for His clothes (Psalm 22:18); the piercing of His side and the fact that His bones were not broken at His death (Zechariah 12:10; Psalm 34:20); and His burial among the rich (Isaiah 53:9).

Perhaps the most beloved of all Old Testament prophecies is encapsulated in the words of Isaiah, who eight centuries before the birth of Christ wrote the following immortal words: "For to us a child is born, to us a son is given, and the government will be on his shoulders. And he will be called *Wonderful Counselor*, *Mighty God*, *Everlasting Father* [possessor of eternity], *Prince of Peace*" (Isaiah 9:6;

emphasis added). Only Messiah, born of a virgin, could match the meaning of such majestic monikers.

Not only so, but the Christ who walked through the doorway of Isaiah's messianic prophecy, made the ultimate prediction: *"Destroy this temple, and I will raise it again in three days. . . .* After he was raised from the dead, his disciples recalled what he had said. *Then they believed* the Scripture and the words that Jesus had spoken" (John 2:19, 22; emphasis added).

Over the years I have discovered time and again that messianic prophecy is the golden key that unlocks the hearts of even hard-boiled skeptics!

READING

For to us a child is born,
　　to us a son is given,
　　and the government will be on his shoulders.
And he will be called
　　Wonderful Counselor, Mighty God,
　　Everlasting Father, Prince of Peace.
Of the increase of his government and peace
　　there will be no end.
He will reign on David's throne
　　and over his kingdom,

establishing and upholding it
> with justice and righteousness
> from that time on and forever.

The zeal of the LORD Almighty
> will accomplish this. (Isaiah 9:6–7)

QUESTIONS

+ How could Daniel, writing six centuries before the time of Christ, have predicted what would happen hundreds of years later?
+ Why are messianic prophecies a golden key that unlocks the hearts of even hardened skeptics?

COME, THOU LONG-EXPECTED JESUS
Charles Wesley

Come, Thou long-expected Jesus,
Born to set Thy people free;
From our fears and sins release us,
Let us find our rest in Thee.
Israel's strength and consolation,
Hope of all the earth Thou art;
Dear desire of every nation,
Joy of every longing heart.

Born Thy people to deliver,
Born a child, and yet a King,
Born to reign in us forever,
Now Thy gracious kingdom bring.
By Thine own eternal Spirit,
Rule in all our hearts alone;
By Thine all-sufficient merit,
Raise us to Thy glorious throne.

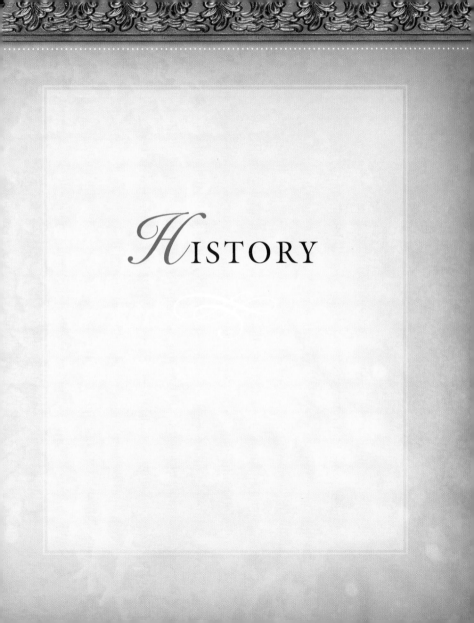

HISTORY

A PAGAN FESTIVAL?

*Therefore do not let anyone judge you by what you eat or drink,
or with regard to a religious festival, a New Moon celebration
or a Sabbath day. These are a shadow of the things that were
to come; the reality, however, is found in Christ.*

—COLOSSIANS 2:16–17

As we continue our journey to the heart of Christmas,
let's pause for a moment to consider a common concern
raised each year regarding the validity of celebrating
Christ's coming—namely, *that when Christmas was originally instituted,
December 25 was a pagan festival commemorating the birthday of a false
god.*

In response we should first acknowledge that this is substantially
true. As noted by Dr. Paul Maier, eminent professor of ancient
history at Western Michigan University, "The Romans of the
time not only celebrated their Saturnalia festival at the close of

December, but they also thought that December 25 marked the date of the winter solstice (instead of December 21), when they observed the pagan feast of *Sol Invictus*, the Unconquerable Sun, which was just in the act of turning about to aim northward once again."

While this is indeed a historical fact, what is frequently overlooked is the reason the early Christian church chose December 25 as their day of celebration. The purpose was not to Christianize a time of pagan revelry, but to establish a rival celebration. As such, Christmas (from Old English *Crīstes* + *mœsse* "Christ's festival") was designated as a spiritually edifying holiday (holy day) on which to proclaim the supremacy of the Son of God over superstitions concerning such gods as Saturn, the god of agriculture, and Sol Invictus, the unconquerable sun god.

While the world has all but forgotten the Greco-Roman gods of antiquity, it is annually reminded that two thousand years ago Christ, the hope of humanity, invaded time and space. But as Christians we perceive an even greater reality. Each year as we celebrate the First Advent of Christ, we are simultaneously reminded of the Second Advent in which the old order of things will pass away and Christ our Lord will put all things to right. As the prophet Zechariah put it, "'Shout and be glad, O Daughter of Zion. For I am coming, and I will live among you,' declares the LORD. 'Many nations will be joined with the LORD in that day and will become my people. I will live among you and you will know that the Lord Almighty has sent me to you'" (2:10–11).

If you cannot celebrate this, pray tell, what can you celebrate?

While Paul was waiting for [Silas and Timothy] in Athens, he was greatly distressed to see that the city was full of idols. So he reasoned in the synagogue with the Jews and the God-fearing Greeks, as well as in the marketplace day by day with those who happened to be there. A group of Epicurean and Stoic philosophers began to dispute with him. Some of them asked, "What is this babbler trying to say?" Others remarked, "He seems to be advocating foreign gods." They said this because Paul was preaching the good news about Jesus and the resurrection. Then they took him and brought him to a meeting of the Areopagus, where they said to him, "May we know what this new teaching is that you are presenting? You are bringing some strange ideas to our ears, and we want to know what they mean." (All the Athenians and the foreigners who lived there spent their time doing nothing but talking about and listening to the latest ideas.)

Paul then stood up in the meeting of the Areopagus and said: "Men of Athens! I see that in every way you are very religious. For as I walked around and looked carefully at your objects of worship, I even found an altar with this inscription: TO AN UNKNOWN GOD . Now what you worship as something unknown I am going to proclaim to you.

"The God who made the world and everything in it is the Lord of heaven and earth and does not live in temples built by hands. And he is not served by human hands, as if he needed anything, because he himself gives all men life and breath and everything else. From one man he made every nation of men, that they should inhabit the whole earth; and he determined the times set for them and the exact places where they should live. God did this so that men would seek him and perhaps reach out for him and find him, though he is not far from each one of us. 'For in him we live and move and have our being.' As some of your own poets have said, 'We are his offspring.'

"Therefore since we are God's offspring, we should not think that the divine being is like gold or silver or stone—an image made by man's design and skill. In the past God overlooked such ignorance, but now he commands all people everywhere to repent. For he has set a day when he will judge the world with justice by the man he has appointed. He has given proof of this to all men by raising him from the dead."

When they heard about the resurrection of the dead, some of them sneered, but others said, "We want to hear you again on this subject." At that, Paul left the Council. A few men became followers of Paul and believed. Among them was Dionysius, a member of the Areopagus, also a woman named Damaris, and a number of others. (Acts 17:16–34)

QUESTIONS

+ Why did the early church choose December 25 to celebrate the birth of Christ?
+ How does the First Advent of Christ ensure that Christ will come again to put all things to right?

ANGELS FROM THE REALMS OF GLORY

James Montgomery

Angels from the realms of glory,
Wing your flight o'er all the earth;
Ye who sang creation's story
Now proclaim Messiah's birth:
Come and worship, come and worship,
Worship Christ, the newborn King.

Shepherds in the field abiding,
Watching o'er your flocks by night,
God with us is now residing;
Yonder shines the infant Light:
Come and worship, come and worship,
Worship Christ, the newborn King.

Sages, leave your contemplations,
Brighter visions beam afar;
Seek the great Desire of nations;
Ye have seen His natal star.
Come and worship, come and worship,
Worship Christ, the newborn King.

Saints, before the altar bending,
Watching long in hope and fear;
Suddenly the Lord, descending,
In His temple shall appear.
Come and worship, come and worship,
Worship Christ, the newborn King.

In the Fullness of Time

But when the time had fully come, God sent his Son,
born of a woman, born under law, to redeem those under law,
that we might receive the full rights of sons.

—Galatians 4:4–5

Jesus Christ, the antitype to which all the types and shadows of the Old Covenant pointed, stands at the very apex of human history. Accordingly, Christmas is not about reveling in mythology; it is about celebrating events that are rooted and grounded in historical fact. As Paul explains, "When the time had fully come, God sent his Son, born of a woman, born under law, to redeem those under law, that we might receive the full rights of sons" (Galatians 4:4–5). As such, the Babe of Bethlehem is the fulfillment of both the law and the prophets. A primary reason why Christians believe in such miracles as Christ's virgin birth is that the Bible is divine rather than merely human in origin.

To begin with, the Bible has stronger manuscript support than any other work of classical history—including Homer, Plato, Aristotle, Caesar, and Tacitus. Equally amazing is the fact that the Bible has been virtually unaltered since the original writing, as is attested to by scholars who have compared the earliest extant manuscripts with manuscripts written centuries later. Additionally, the reliability of the Bible is affirmed by the testimony of its authors, who were eyewitnesses—or close associates of eyewitnesses—to the recorded events, and by ancient secular historians who confirm the many events, people, places, and customs chronicled in Scripture.

Furthermore, archaeology is a powerful witness to the accuracy of the New Testament documents. Repeatedly, comprehensive archaeological fieldwork and careful biblical interpretation affirm the reliability of the Bible. For example, recent archaeological finds have corroborated biblical details surrounding the trial that led to the fatal torment of Jesus Christ—including Pontius Pilate, who ordered Christ's crucifixion, as well as Caiaphas, the high priest who presided over the religious trials of Christ. It is telling when secular scholars must revise their biblical criticisms in light of solid archaeological evidence.

Finally, the Bible records predictions of events that could not be known or predicted by chance or common sense. For example, against all odds, Jesus predicted the destruction of Jerusalem and the Jewish temple within a generation—a prophecy fulfilled by the

Roman General Titus in AD 70. It is statistically preposterous that any or all of the Bible's specific, detailed prophecies could have been fulfilled through chance, good guessing, or deliberate deceit.

Today, as you ponder the heart of Christmas, be assured that the Scriptures that chronicle the historical certainty of Christ's coming in flesh are demonstratably rooted in both history and solid evidence.

READING

What I am saying is that as long as the heir is a child, he is no different from a slave, although he owns the whole estate. He is subject to guardians and trustees until the time set by his father. So also, when we were children, we were in slavery under the basic principles of the world. But when the time had fully come, God sent his Son, born of a woman, born under law, to redeem those under law, that we might receive the full rights of sons. Because you are sons, God sent the Spirit of his Son into our hearts, the Spirit who calls out, "*Abba*, Father." So you are no longer a slave, but a son; and since you are a son, God has made you also an heir. (Galatians 4:1–7)

QUESTIONS

+ How would you defend the Bible as divine rather than merely human in origin?
+ How does archaeology support the historicity of the Bible?

I Heard the Bells on Christmas Day

Henry W. Longfellow

I heard the bells on Christmas Day
Their old familiar carols play,
And wild and sweet the words repeat
Of peace on earth, good will to men.

I thought how, as the day had come,
The belfries of all Christendom
Had rolled along the unbroken song
Of peace on earth, good will to men.

And in despair I bowed my head:
"There is no peace on earth," I said,
"For hate is strong, and mocks the song
Of peace on earth, good will to men."

Then pealed the bells more loud and deep:
"God is not dead, nor doth He sleep;
The wrong shall fail, the right prevail
With peace on earth, good will to men."

Till, ringing, singing on its way,
The world revolved from night to day
A voice, a chime, a chant sublime,
Of peace on earth, good will to men.

GENEALOGIES OF THE BABE OF BETHLEHEM

*A record of the genealogy of Jesus Christ the
son of David, the son of Abraham.*

—MATTHEW 1:1

Despite the wealth of evidence that supports the historical reliability of the Gospels, some scholars point to apparent inconsistencies as evidence of their unreliability. One of the most frequently cited contradictions involves the genealogies of Jesus as recorded in Matthew and Luke. At first blush the genealogies of Matthew and Luke may appear to be contradictory; in reality, however, they are ingeniously constructed to highlight different aspects of the person and work of Jesus Christ.

Matthew, writing to a primarily Jewish audience, emphasizes that Jesus Christ is the seed of Abraham and the legal heir of David, the long-awaited King of Israel who would ultimately restore His people from exile. As such, Matthew records fourteen generations from Abraham to David, fourteen from David to the exile, and fourteen from the exile to the Christ (Matthew 1:17). Matthew, a former tax collector, skillfully organizes the genealogy of Jesus into three groups of fourteen, the numerical equivalent of the Hebrew letters in King David's name ($D+V+D$ = 4+6+4). Thus, Matthew's genealogy simultaneously highlights the most significant names in the lineage of Jesus and artistically emphasizes our Lord's identity as Messiah who would forever sit upon the throne of David.

Luke, writing to a primarily Gentile audience, extends his genealogy past Abraham to the First Adam, thus highlighting that Christ, the Second Adam, is the Savior of all humanity. Additionally, calling Adam "the son of God" and strategically placing the genealogy between Jesus' baptism and the desert temptation, Luke masterfully reveals Jesus as *Theanthropos*—the God-man. It is also instructive to note that while Luke's genealogy stretches from the First Adam to the Second, only mountain peaks in the lineage are accounted for. Thus, it is impossible to determine how many years elapsed between the creation of Adam and the birth of Jesus.

Just as there are different emphases in the genealogies, so too there are different explanations for the dissimilarities between them. Matthew traces his genealogy through David's son Solomon, while Luke traces his genealogy through David's son Nathan. It may be that Matthew's purpose is to provide the legal lineage from Solomon through Joseph, while Luke's purpose is to provide the natural lineage from Nathan through Mary. It could also be that Matthew and Luke are both tracing Joseph's genealogy—Matthew, the legal line, and Luke, the natural line. As such, the legal line diverges from the natural in that Levirate Law stipulated if a man died without an heir, his genealogy could legally continue through his brother (Deuteronomy 25:5–6). The fact that there are a number of ways to resolve dissimilarities rules out the notion that the genealogies are contradictory.

As you read through the genealogies of Jesus on Day 5 of your journey toward Christmas Day, may they remind you that the Babe of Bethlehem is a real, historical person, who was miraculously conceived in the womb of the Virgin Mary and ultimately raised from a tomb in Jerusalem so that you and I can experience rebirth and resurrection.

READING

Paul, a servant of Christ Jesus, called to be an apostle and set apart for the gospel of God—the gospel he promised beforehand through his prophets in the Holy Scriptures regarding his Son, who as to his human nature was a descendant of David, and who through the Spirit of holiness was declared with power to be the Son of God by his resurrection from the dead: Jesus Christ our Lord. Through him and for his name's sake, we received grace and apostleship to call people from among all the Gentiles to the obedience that comes from faith. And you also are among those who are called to belong to Jesus Christ. (Romans 1:1–6)

QUESTIONS

+ Are the genealogies in Matthew and Luke contradictory?
+ What are some ways to resolve dissimilarities between Matthew's and Luke's genealogies?

WHILE SHEPHERDS WATCHED
Nahum Tate

While shepherds watched their flocks by night,
All seated on the ground,
The angel of the Lord came down,
And glory shone around,
And glory shone around.

"Fear not," said he, for mighty dread
Had seized their troubled mind,
"Glad tidings of great joy I bring,
To you and all mankind,
To you and all mankind.

"To you, in David's town, this day
Is born of David's line,
The Savior, who is Christ the Lord,
And this shall be the sign,
And this shall be the sign.

"The heavenly Babe you there shall find
To human view displayed,

All meanly wrapped in swathing bands,
And in a manger laid,
And in a manger laid."

Thus spake the seraph and forthwith
Appeared a shining throng
Of angels praising God on high,
Addressed their joyful song,
Addressed their joyful song:

"All glory be to God on high,
And to the earth be peace;
Good will henceforth from heaven to men
Begin and never cease,
Begin and never cease!"

CENSUS CONSIDERATIONS

> *In those days Caesar Augustus issued a decree that a census*
> *should be taken of the entire Roman world. (This was the first*
> *census that took place while Quirinius was governor of Syria.)*
> *And everyone went to his own town to register.*
>
> —LUKE 2:1–3

On the *Dateline NBC*'s "The Birth of Jesus" episode, Dr. John Dominic Crossan, co-founder of the wildly popular Jesus Seminar, called into question the historical veracity of Holy Scripture. Said Crossan: "Luke tells us the story that at the time *Jesus was born* Augustus had decreed a census of the whole earth. *Now, every scholar will tell you there was no such census ever.*"

Is Crossan correct? Is the Canon corrupt? Did Dr. Luke make a colossal historical blunder that effectively discredits sacred Scripture? In an age in which the historical reliability of the Bible is being questioned, it is crucial that Christians are equipped to demonstrate that Scripture is the *infallible* repository of redemptive revelation. So how do we respond to critics like Crossan? Is his pontification on NBC a defensible argument or merely a dogmatic assertion?

First, while Crossan made his pontification with typical bravado, it turns out to be patently false. Caesar Augustus was famous for census taking. So famous, in fact, that this issue is no longer even debated among credible historians. The Jewish historian Josephus refers to a Roman taxation in AD 6, and considering the scope of the taxation, it is logical to assume that it took a long time to complete. Undoubtedly it began with Caesar Augustus around 5 BC and was likely completed a decade later.

Furthermore, Luke—ever the meticulous historian—notes that the census took place when Quirinius served as governor of Syria. As Paul Maier, an esteemed professor of ancient history at Western Michigan University, noted on the *Bible Answer Man* broadcast, the Romans took forty years to get a census done in Gaul, so for a province fifteen hundred miles away from Rome to take a decade is eminently reasonable. Moreover, since the census came in under the administration of Quirinius, it would correctly be labeled as such. Not only so, but given Luke's impeccable credentials as a historian, it would have been far more circumspect for Crossan to temper his dogmatism.

Finally, one need only remember the experience of the brilliant archaeologist Sir William Ramsay, who, like Crossan, was bent on undermining Luke's historical reliability. Through his painstaking Mediterranean archaeological adventures, he discovered that, one after the other, the historical allusions that Luke provides are accurate. If, as Ramsay points out, Luke does not err in referencing a plethora of countries, cities, islands, and all the details surrounding them, then there's no reason to doubt him concerning the census.

On Day 7 of your historic journey to the birthplace of Jesus, why not make a commitment to "always be prepared to give an answer to everyone who asks you to give the reason for the hope that you have" (1 Peter 3:15)? And remember, even if you don't have the answer at your fingertips, you can always research and return.

May God use your well-reasoned answers this Christmas season as an opportunity to share the grace and truth and light that only the Christ of Christmas can bring to the human heart.

READING

But you, Bethlehem Ephrathah,
    though you are small among the clans of Judah,
out of you will come for me
    one who will be ruler over Israel,
whose origins are from of old,
    from ancient times. (Micah 5:2)

In those days Caesar Augustus issued a decree that a census should be taken of the entire Roman world. (This was the first census that took place while Quirinius was governor of Syria.) And everyone went to his own town to register.

So Joseph also went up from the town of Nazareth in Galilee to Judea, to Bethlehem the town of David, because he belonged to the house and line of David. He went there to register with Mary, who was pledged to be married to him and was expecting a child. While they were there, the time came for the baby to be born, and she gave birth to her firstborn, a son. She wrapped him in cloths and placed him in a manger, because there was no room for them in the inn. (Luke 2:1–7)

QUESTIONS

+ In what way is Crossan's pontification a dogmatic assertion rather than a defensible argument?
+ Why did Sir William Ramsay conclude that Dr. Luke was a reliable historian?

O LITTLE TOWN OF BETHLEHEM

Phillips Brooks

O little town of Bethlehem, how still we see thee lie!
Above thy deep and dreamless sleep the silent stars go by.
Yet in thy dark streets shineth the everlasting Light;
The hopes and fears of all the years are met in thee tonight.

For Christ is born of Mary, and gathered all above,
While mortals sleep, the angels keep their watch of wondering love.
O morning stars together proclaim the holy birth,
And praises sing to God the King, and peace to men on earth!

How silently, how silently, the wondrous gift is giv'n;
So God imparts to human hearts the blessings of His heav'n.
No ear may hear His coming, but in this world of sin,
Where meek souls will receive Him still, the dear Christ enters in.

O holy Child of Bethlehem, descend to us, we pray;
Cast out our sin, and enter in; be born in us today.
We hear the Christmas angels the great glad tidings tell;
O come to us, abide with us, our Lord Emmanuel!

RESURRECTION

TIDINGS OF COMFORT AND JOY

For what I received I passed on to you as of first importance: that Christ died for our sins according to the Scriptures, that he was buried, that he was raised on the third day according to the Scriptures, and that he appeared to Peter, and then to the Twelve. After that, he appeared to more than five hundred of the brothers at the same time, most of whom are still living, though some have fallen asleep. Then he appeared to James, then to all the apostles, and last of all he appeared to me also, as to one abnormally born.

—1 CORINTHIANS 15:3–8

Without the resurrection of Jesus, there is little point in even discussing Christmas. As the apostle Paul put it in a letter to the Corinthian Christians, "If Christ has not been raised, our preaching is useless and so is your faith" (1 Corinthians 15:14). In light of Paul's words, it is incumbent on Christians to demonstrate that the Christ of Christmas had the power to lay down His life and the power to take it up again, thus demonstrating that He is God in human flesh (cf. John 2:19).

To begin with, liberal and conservative scholars alike concede that after suffering fatal torment, Jesus was buried in the private tomb of Joseph of Arimathea. Philosopher William Lane Craig points out that as a member of the Jewish court that condemned Jesus to death, Joseph of Arimathea is unlikely to be Christian fiction (Mark 15:43). Moreover, Craig notes that Jesus' burial is substantiated by Mark's gospel (15:46) and is, therefore, reported far too early to have been the subject of legendary corruption. Indeed, the earliest Jewish response to the resurrection of Christ presupposes the empty tomb (Matthew 28:11–13), and in the centuries following the resurrection, the fact of the empty tomb was forwarded by Jesus' friends and foes alike. In short, early Christianity could not have survived an identifiable tomb containing the corpse of Christ.[1]

Furthermore, Jesus gave His disciples many convincing proofs that He had risen from the dead. Paul, for example, points out that Christ "appeared to more than five hundred of the brothers at the same time, most of whom are still living, though some have fallen asleep" (1 Corinthians 15:6). It would have been one thing to attribute these supernatural experiences to people who had already died. It was quite another to attribute them to multitudes who were still alive. As the famed New Testament scholar of Cambridge University C. H. Dodd points out, "There can hardly be any purpose in mentioning the fact that most of the five hundred are still alive, unless Paul is saying, in effect, 'The witnesses are there to be questioned.'"[2]

Finally, what happened as a result of the resurrection is unprecedented in human history. In the span of a few hundred years, a small band of seemingly insignificant believers succeeded in turning an entire empire upside down. While it is conceivable that they would have faced torture, vilification, and even cruel deaths for what they fervently believed to be true, it is inconceivable that they would have been willing to die for what they knew to be a lie. As Dr. Simon Greenleaf, the famous Royal Professor of Law at Harvard, put it: "If it were morally possible for them to have been deceived in this matter, every human motive operated to lead them to discover and avow their error. . . . If then their testimony was not true, there was no possible motive for this fabrication."[3]

Given the rock-solid evidence for the central pillar on which Christianity either rises or falls, we can with great certainty embrace Christ's miraculous conception in the womb of the Virgin Mary.

✧ ─────────── | READING | ─────────── ✧

But if it is preached that Christ has been raised from the dead, how can some of you say that there is no resurrection of the dead? If there is no resurrection of the dead, then not even Christ has been raised. And if Christ has not been raised, our preaching is useless and so is your faith. More than that, we are then found to be false witnesses about God, for we have testified about God that he raised Christ from the dead. But he did not raise him if in fact the dead are not raised. For if the dead are not raised, then Christ has not been raised either. And if Christ has not been raised, your faith is futile; you are still in your sins. Then those also who have fallen asleep in Christ are lost. If only for this life we have hope in Christ, we are to be pitied more than all men.

But Christ has indeed been raised from the dead, the firstfruits of those who have fallen asleep. (1 Corinthians 15:12–20)

QUESTIONS

+ Why is the subject of the resurrection so important in telling the Christmas story?
+ What evidence is there for Christ's resurrection?

GOD REST YE MERRY, GENTLEMEN
Traditional English Carol

God rest ye merry, gentlemen, let nothing you dismay,
Remember Christ our Savior was born on Christmas Day;
To save us all from Satan's power when we were gone astray.
O tidings of comfort and joy, comfort and joy;
O tidings of comfort and joy.

In Bethlehem, in Jewry, this blessed Babe was born,
And laid within a manger upon this blessed morn;
The which His mother Mary did nothing take in scorn.
O tidings of comfort and joy, comfort and joy;
O tidings of comfort and joy.

From God our heavenly Father a blessed angel came;
And unto certain shepherds brought tidings of the same;
How that in Bethlehem was born the Son of God by name.
O tidings of comfort and joy, comfort and joy;
O tidings of comfort and joy.

INCARNATION

Day 9

IMMANUEL

In Christ all the fullness of the Deity lives in bodily form.

—COLOSSIANS 2:9

The reason we rejoice at Christmas is that the Baby born to Mary and Joseph on the first Advent was no ordinary child. As Matthew records, this Baby was the ultimate fulfillment of Isaiah's prophecy of Immanuel—"God with us" (Matthew 1:22–23). The ultimate self-revelation of God to humankind, Jesus the Christ was and eternally is God incarnate (literally, "in flesh").

Although John's gospel does not include a narrative of the birth and infancy of Jesus, the doctrine of the incarnation is aptly summed up in his introduction: "In the beginning was the Word, and the Word was with God, and the Word was God. . . . The Word became flesh and made his dwelling among us. We have seen his glory, the glory of the One and Only, who came from the Father, full of grace and truth" (John 1:1, 14).

The clear testimony of Scripture is that, in the incarnation, Jesus Christ was fully God and fully man; that is, He existed as the perfect unity in one person of a divine and a human nature. Paul eloquently expressed the profound truth of the incarnation in his letter to the Philippian Christians saying: "Your attitude should be the same as that of Christ Jesus: Who, being in very nature God, did not consider equality with God something to be grasped, but made himself nothing, taking the very nature of a servant, being made in human likeness. And being found in appearance as a man, he humbled himself and became obedient to death—even death on a cross" (Philippians 2:5–8).

As *Theanthropos* ("God-Man"), the spotless "Lamb of God" (John 1:29) lived a perfectly sinless human life and died a sinner's death to sufficiently atone, once and for all, for the sins of humanity (Romans 5:1–21; Hebrews 10:11–18). Without both natures, Christ's payment would have been insufficient. As God, His sacrifice was sufficient to provide redemption for the sins of humankind. As man, He did what the first Adam failed to do. Says Paul, "For just as through the disobedience of the one man the many were made sinners, so also through the obedience of the one man the many will be made righteous" (Romans 5:19). Or, as Paul explained to the Corinthians, "As in Adam all die, so in Christ all will be made alive" (1 Corinthians 15:22).

Your attitude should be the same as that of Christ Jesus:

    Who, being in very nature God,

        did not consider equality with God something to be grasped,

    but made himself nothing,

        taking the very nature of a servant,

        being made in human likeness.

    And being found in appearance as a man,

        he humbled himself

        and became obedient to death—

            even death on a cross!

    Therefore God exalted him to the highest place

        and gave him the name that is above every name,

    that at the name of Jesus every knee should bow,

        in heaven and on earth and under the earth,

    and every tongue confess that Jesus Christ is Lord,

        to the glory of God the Father. (Philippians 2:5–11)

+ What makes the Child of Mary special?
+ Why was it necessary for God to be incarnated as the *Theanthropos* or "God-Man"?

O Come, O Come Emmanuel

Translation by John Mason Neale

O come, O come, Emmanuel, and ransom captive Israel,
That mourns in lonely exile here until the Son of God appear.
Rejoice! Rejoice! Emmanuel shall come to thee, O Israel.

O come, Thou Rod of Jesse, free Thine
own from Satan's tyranny;
From depths of hell Thy people save, and give
them victory o'er the grave.
Rejoice! Rejoice! Emmanuel shall come to thee, O Israel.

O come, Thou Day-Spring come and cheer,
our spirits by Thine advent here;
Disperse the gloomy clouds of night, and death's
dark shadows put to flight.
Rejoice! Rejoice! Emmanuel shall come to thee, O Israel.

O come, Thou Key of David, come, and open
wide our heavenly home;
Make safe the way that leads on high, and close
the path to misery.

Rejoice! Rejoice! Emmanuel shall come to thee, O Israel.

O come, O come, great Lord of might, who to
Thy tribes on Sinai's height,
In ancient times once gave the law in cloud and majesty and awe.
Rejoice! Rejoice! Emmanuel shall come to thee, O Israel.

ONE PERSON—TWO NATURES

In the beginning was the Word, and the Word was with God,
and the Word was God. . . . The Word became flesh and made his dwelling
among us. We have seen his glory, the glory of the One and Only,
who came from the Father, full of grace and truth.

—JOHN 1:1, 14

Like the Trinity, the doctrine of the incarnation is often considered to be logically incoherent. While many issues surrounding the incarnation, such as the precise modes of interaction between Christ's divine nature and His human nature, may transcend our human understanding, the doctrine of the incarnation does not transgress the laws of logic.

To understand the logical coherence of the incarnation, one must first consider the *imago Dei* (image of God). Because God created humanity in His own image (Genesis 1:27), the essential properties of human nature (rationality, will, moral character, and the like) are not inconsistent with His divine nature. While the notion of God becoming a clam would be absurd, the reality that God became a man is not.

Furthermore, it is crucial to point out that though the God-Man is *fully* human, He is not *merely* human. Though He took on all the essential properties of human nature, He did not take on that which is nonessential (e.g., sinful inclinations). Indeed, as Adam was created without a proclivity toward sin, so the Second Adam was untainted by original sin. As with His moral perfection, Jesus' other divine attributes (omniscience, omnipotence, omnipresence, and so forth) were not undermined in the incarnation.

Finally, while Jesus Christ voluntarily refrained from exercising certain attributes of deity, He did not divest Himself of a single divine attribute (John 1:14; Philippians 2:1–11; Colossians 1:15–20; Hebrew 2:14–18). With respect to His omniscience, for example, His human nature may have served as a filter limiting His knowledge as a man (e.g., Mark 13:32). Nonetheless, Jesus' divine omniscience was ever accessible at the will of the Father.

In sum, there is no incoherence in the biblical teaching that Jesus became and will forever remain one person with two distinct natures—neither commingling His natures nor becoming two persons. It is this miraculous incarnation of God that you and I, along with Christians around the world, corporately celebrate this Christmas season.

In the beginning was the Word, and the Word was with God, and the Word was God. He was with God in the beginning.

Through him all things were made; without him nothing was made that has been made. In him was life, and that life was the light of men. The light shines in the darkness, but the darkness has not understood it.

There came a man who was sent from God; his name was John. He came as a witness to testify concerning that light, so that through him all men might believe. He himself was not the light; he came only as a witness to the light. The true light that gives light to every man was coming into the world.

He was in the world, and though the world was made through him, the world did not recognize him. He came to that which was his own, but his own did not receive him. Yet to all who received him, to those who believed in his name, he gave the right to become children of God—children born not of natural descent, nor of human decision or a husband's will, but born of God.

The Word became flesh and made his dwelling among us. We have seen his glory, the glory of the One and Only, who came from the Father, full of grace and truth.

John testifies concerning him. He cries out, saying, "This was he of whom I said, 'He who comes after me has surpassed me because he was before me.'" From the fullness of his grace we have all received one blessing after another. For the law was given through Moses; grace and truth came through Jesus Christ. No one has ever seen God, but God the One and Only, who is at the Father's side, has made him known. (John 1:1–18)

QUESTIONS

+ In what ways is Jesus fully human? In what ways is He fully God?
+ Did becoming a man make Jesus lose any of His divine attributes? Explain.

ONCE IN ROYAL DAVID'S CITY

Cecil Frances Humphreys Alexander

Once in royal David's city stood a lowly cattle shed,
Where a mother laid her Baby in a manger for His bed;
Mary was that mother mild, Jesus Christ, her little Child.

He came down to earth from heaven, who is God and Lord of all,
And His shelter was a stable, and His cradle was a stall;
With the poor, and mean, and lowly, lived on earth our Savior holy.

And, through all His wondrous childhood,
He would honor and obey,
Love and watch the lowly maiden, in whose gentle arms He lay:
Christian children all must be mild, obedient, good as He.

And our eyes at last shall see Him, through His own redeeming love,
For that Child so dear and gentle is our Lord in heav'n above,
And He leads His children on to the place where He is gone.

Not in that poor lowly stable, with the oxen standing by,
We shall see Him; but in heaven, set at God's right had on high;
When like stars His children crowned all in white shall wait around.

DID THE CHRIST OF CHRISTMAS CLAIM TO BE GOD?

I am the First and the Last. I am the Living One; I was dead,
and behold I am alive for ever and ever!

—REVELATION 1:17B–18A

When Jesus came to Caesarea Philippi, He asked His disciples the mother of all questions, *"Who do you say I am?"* (Matthew 16:15; Mark 8:29; Luke 9:20). Mormons answer the question by saying that Jesus is the spirit brother of Lucifer; Jehovah's Witnesses say that Jesus was the archangel Michael who appeared in the incarnation as merely human; New Agers say Jesus was an avatar, or messenger. Jesus, however, demonstrated that in the incarnation He was undiminished deity.

First, Jesus claimed to be the unique Son of God. As a result, the Jewish leaders tried to kill Him because in "calling God his own Father, [Jesus was] making himself equal with God" (John 5:18). In

John 8:58 Jesus went so far as to use the very words by which God revealed Himself to Moses from the burning bush (Exodus 3:14). To the Jews this was the epitome of blasphemy, for they knew that in doing so Jesus was clearly claiming to be God. On yet another occasion, Jesus explicitly told the Jews, "'I and the Father are one.' Again the Jews picked up stones to stone him, but Jesus said to them, 'I have shown you many great miracles from the Father. For which of these do you stone me?' 'We are not stoning you for any of these,' replied the Jews, 'but for blasphemy, because you, a mere man, claim to be God'" (John 10:30–33).

Furthermore, Jesus made an unmistakable claim to deity before the chief priests and the whole Sanhedrin. Caiaphas the high priest asked Him, "'Are you the Christ, the Son of the Blessed One?' 'I am,' said Jesus, 'And you will see the Son of Man sitting at the right hand of the Mighty One and coming on the clouds of heaven'" (Mark 14:61–62). A biblically illiterate person might well have missed the import of Jesus' words. Caiaphas and the Council, however, did not. They knew that in saying He was "the *Son of Man*" who would come "*on the clouds of heaven*," He was making an overt reference to "the *son of man*" in Daniel's prophecy (Daniel 7:13–14). In doing so, He was not only claiming to be the preexistent Sovereign of the Universe, but prophesying that He would vindicate His claim by judging the very court that was now condemning Him. Moreover, by combining

Daniel's prophecy with David's proclamation in Psalm 110, Jesus was claiming that He would sit on the throne of Israel's God and share God's very glory. To students of the Old Testament, this was the height of "blasphemy," so "they all condemned him as worthy of death" (Mark 14:64).

Finally, during the incarnation, Jesus claimed to possess the very attributes of God. For example, He claimed *omniscience* by telling Peter, "This very night, before the rooster crows, you will disown me three times" (Matthew 26:34). Jesus declared *omnipotence* by not only resurrecting Lazarus (John 11:43), but by raising Himself from the dead (see John 2:19), and Jesus professed *omnipresence* by promising He would be with His disciples "to the very end of the age" (Matthew 28:20). Not only so, but Jesus said to the paralytic in Luke 5:20, "Friend, your sins are forgiven." As such, He claimed a prerogative reserved for God alone.

Today as we contemplate the mother of all questions, may we evermore be mindful that the Christ born in a manger is the very One who spoke and caused the limitless galaxies to leap into existence.

⟶ ——————————| READING |—————————— ⟵

"This is what the LORD says—

Israel's King and Redeemer, the LORD Almighty:
I am the first and I am the last;
    apart from me there is no God.
Who then is like me? Let him proclaim it.
    Let him declare and lay out before me
what has happened since I established my ancient people,
    and what is yet to come—
    yes, let him foretell what will come.
Do not tremble, do not be afraid.
    Did I not proclaim this and foretell it long ago?
You are my witnesses. Is there any God besides me?
    No, there is no other Rock; I know not one." (Isaiah 44:6-8)

"Behold, I am coming soon! My reward is with me, and I will give to
everyone according to what he has done. I am the Alpha and the
Omega, the First and the Last, the Beginning and the End."
(Revelation 22:12–13)

QUESTIONS

+ In what ways do people misidentify Jesus?
+ What is so significant about Jesus identifying Himself as the
  "Son of Man"?

CROWN HIM

Matthew Bridges and Godfrey Thring

Crown Him with many crowns, the Lamb upon His throne.
Hark! How the heavenly anthem drowns all music but its own.
Awake, my soul, and sing of Him who died for thee,
And hail Him as thy matchless King through all eternity.

Crown Him the virgin's Son, the God incarnate born,
Whose arm those crimson trophies won which now His brow adorn;
Fruit of the mystic rose, as of that rose the stem;
The root whence mercy ever flows, the Babe of Bethlehem.

Crown Him the Lord of life, who triumphed o'er the grave,
And rose victorious in the strife for those He came to save.
His glories now we sing, who died, and rose on high,
Who died eternal life to bring, and lives that death may die.

Crown Him the Lord of love, behold His hands and side,
Those wounds, yet visible above, in beauty glorified.
No angel in the sky can fully bear that sight,
But downward bends his burning eye at mysteries so bright.

Crown Him the Lord of Heaven, enthroned in worlds above,
Crown Him the King to whom is given the wondrous name of Love.
Crown Him with many crowns, as thrones before Him fall;
Crown Him, ye kings, with many crowns, for He is King of all.

WHAT CHILD IS THIS?

When John heard in prison what Christ was doing, he sent his disciples to ask
him, "Are you the one who was to come, or should we expect someone else?"
Jesus replied, "Go back and report to John what you hear and see:
The blind receive sight, the lame walk, those who have leprosy are cured,
the deaf hear, the dead are raised, and the good news is preached to the poor.
Blessed is the man who does not fall away on account of me."

—MATTHEW 11:2–6

I t is one thing to say that the child born in Bethlehem was God
incarnate; it is quite another to establish it beyond a reasonable
doubt. To do so, we must demonstrate Jesus to be the sinless,
supernatural Savior of humanity.

First, Christ is the only human who ever demonstrated the
credential of sinlessness. While the Qur'an exhorts Muhammad to
seek forgiveness for his sins or faults (40:55; 47:19; cf. 48:1–3), the Bible
exonerates Messiah, saying Jesus "had no sin" (2 Corinthians 5:21).
And this is no singular statement. John declares, "And in him is no sin"

(1 John 3:5), and Peter says Jesus "committed no sin, and no deceit was found in his mouth" (1 Peter 2:22). Jesus Himself went so far as to challenge His antagonists asking, "Can any of you prove me guilty of sin?" (John 8:46).

Furthermore, Jesus demonstrated supernatural authority over sickness, the forces of nature, fallen angels, and even death itself. Matthew 4 records that Jesus went throughout Galilee teaching, preaching, "and healing every disease and sickness among the people" (v. 23). Mark 4 documents Jesus rebuking the winds and the waves saying, "Quiet! Be still!" (v. 39). In Luke 4 Jesus encounters a man possessed by an evil spirit and commands the demon to "Come out of him!" (v. 35). And in John 4, Jesus tells the royal official whose son was close to death, "Your son will live" (v. 50). In fact, the four Gospel writers all records that Jesus demonstrated ultimate power over death through the immutable fact of His resurrection.

Finally, the credentials of Christ's deity are seen in the lives of countless men, women, and children. Each day, people of every tongue and tribe and nation experience the Christ of Christmas by repenting of their sins and receiving Him as Lord and Savior of their lives. Thus, they not only come to know about Christ evidentially, but experientially as Christ becomes more real to them than the very flesh on their bones.

What Child is this? None other than the sinless, supernatural Savior "who was conceived by the Holy Ghost, born of the Virgin Mary; suffered under Pontius Pilate, was crucified, dead, and buried . . . the third day He rose again from the dead; He ascended into heaven, and sitteth on the right hand of God the Father Almighty; from thence He shall come to judge the quick and the dead."

READING

The desert and the parched land will be glad;
    the wilderness will rejoice and blossom.
Like the crocus, it will burst into bloom;
    it will rejoice greatly and shout for joy.
The glory of Lebanon will be given to it,
    the splendor of Carmel and Sharon;
they will see the glory of the LORD,
    the splendor of our God.

Strengthen the feeble hands,
    steady the knees that give way;
say to those with fearful hearts,
    "Be strong, do not fear;
your God will come,
    he will come with vengeance;

with divine retribution
>
> he will come to save you."

Then will the eyes of the blind be opened
>
> and the ears of the deaf unstopped.
>
> Then will the lame leap like a deer,
>
> and the mute tongue shout for joy.
>
> Water will gush forth in the wilderness
>
> and streams in the desert. (Isaiah 35:1–6)

Jesus went throughout Galilee, teaching in their synagogues, preaching the good news of the kingdom, and healing every disease and sickness among the people. News about him spread all over Syria, and people brought to him all who were ill with various diseases, those suffering severe pain, the demon-possessed, those having seizures, and the paralyzed, and he healed them. Large crowds from Galilee, the Decapolis, Jerusalem, Judea and the region across the Jordan followed him. (Matthew 4:23–25)

QUESTIONS

+ How is Jesus different than Muhammad?
+ What works did Christ perform to support His claim to be God?

WHAT CHILD IS THIS? (GREENSLEEVES)

William Chatterton Dix

What child is this who, laid to rest,
On Mary's lap is sleeping?
Whom angels greet with anthems sweet,
While shepherds watch are keeping?
This, this is Christ the King,
Whom shepherds guard and angels sing;
Haste, haste to bring Him laud,
The Babe, the Son of Mary.

Why lies He in such mean estate
Where ox and ass are feeding?
Good Christian, fear; for sinners here
The silent Word is pleading;
Nails, spear, shall pierce Him through,
The cross be borne for me, for you.
Hail, hail the Word made flesh,
The babe, the Son of Mary.

So bring Him incense, gold, and myrrh,
Come peasant, king to own Him;

The King of kings salvation brings,
Let loving hearts enthrone Him.
Raise, raise the song on high,
The Virgin sings her lullaby.
Joy, joy for Christ is born,
The Babe, the Son of Mary.

THE PREEMINENT CHRIST

[Jesus Christ] is the image of the invisible God, the firstborn over all creation.
—COLOSSIANS 1:15

Not everyone who believes in the virgin birth account is committed to the essential that Jesus was conceived as God incarnate. Jehovah's Witnesses, for example, hold that Jesus was created by God as the archangel Michael, during His earthly sojourn became merely human, and after His crucifixion was re-created as an immaterial spirit creature. Moreover, the Witnesses use Colossians 1:15 as a pretext for the notion that Jesus was the first and greatest creation of Jehovah prior to the creation of the world. All of this begs the question, was Jesus conceived by the Virgin Mary as God in human flesh? And, how can Christ be both the eternal Creator of all things and yet Himself be *firstborn*?

First, in referring to Christ as the *firstborn*, Paul has in mind preeminence. This usage is firmly established in the Old Testament. For example, Ephraim is referred to as the Lord's "firstborn"

(Jeremiah 31:9) even though Manasseh was born first (Genesis 41:51). Likewise, David is appointed the Lord's "firstborn, the most exalted of the kings of the earth" (Psalm 89:27) despite being the youngest of Jesse's sons (1 Samuel 16:10–13). While neither Ephraim nor David was the first one born in his family, both were firstborn in the sense of preeminence or prime position.

Furthermore, Paul refers to Jesus as the firstborn *over* all creation, not the firstborn *in* creation. As such, "He is before *all things* and in him *all things* hold together" (Colossians 1:17; emphasis added). The force of Paul's language is such that the cult of Jehovah's Witnesses, who subscribe to the ancient Arian heresy that the Son is not preexistent and co-eternal with the Father, have been forced to insert the word *other* (e.g., "all other things") in their deeply flawed New World Translation of the Bible in order to demote Christ to the status of a created being.

Finally, as the panoply of Scripture makes plain, Jesus is the eternal Creator who spoke and the limitless galaxies leapt into existence. In John 1, He is overtly called "God" (v. 1), and in Hebrews 1, He is said to be the One who "laid the foundations of the earth" (v. 10). And in the very last chapter of the Bible, Christ refers to Himself as "the Alpha and the Omega, the First and the Last, the Beginning and the End" (Revelation 22:13; cf. Isaiah 44:6; 48:12). Indeed, the whole of Scripture precludes the possibility that the Christ born of a virgin could be anything other than the preexistent Sovereign of the universe.

For [Jesus Christ] has rescued us from the dominion of darkness and brought us into the kingdom of the Son he loves, in whom we have redemption, the forgiveness of sins.

He is the image of the invisible God, the firstborn over all creation. For by him all things were created: things in heaven and on earth, visible and invisible, whether thrones or powers or rulers or authorities; all things were created by him and for him. He is before all things, and in him all things hold together. And he is the head of the body, the church; he is the beginning and the firstborn from among the dead, so that in everything he might have the supremacy. For God was pleased to have all his fullness dwell in him, and through him to reconcile to himself all things, whether things on earth or things in heaven, by making peace through his blood, shed on the cross. (Colossians 1:13–20)

QUESTIONS

+ What is the biblical meaning of the word *firstborn*?
+ Why is it so crucial to read Scripture in its context as opposed to using isolated texts as pretexts for pet theories or theologies?

ALL HAIL THE POWER OF JESUS' NAME
Edward Perronet

All hail the power of Jesus' name! Let angels prostrate fall;
Bring forth the royal diadem, and crown Him Lord of all.
Bring forth the royal diadem, and crown Him Lord of all.

Let highborn seraphs tune the lyre, and as they tune it, fall
Before His face who tunes their choir, and crown Him Lord of all.
Before His face who tunes their choir, and crown Him Lord of all.

Crown Him, ye morning stars of light, who fixed this floating ball;
Now hail the strength of Israel's might, and crown Him Lord of all.
Now hail the strength of Israel's might, and crown Him Lord of all.

Crown Him, ye martyrs of your God, who from His altar call;
Extol the Stem of Jesse's Rod, and crown Him Lord of all.
Extol the Stem of Jesse's Rod, and crown Him Lord of all.

Ye seed of Israel's chosen race, ye ransomed from the fall,
Hail Him who saves you by His grace, and crown Him Lord of all.
Hail Him who saves you by His grace, and crown Him Lord of all.

Hail Him, ye heirs of David's line, whom David Lord did call,
The God incarnate, Man divine, and crown Him Lord of all,
The God incarnate, Man divine, and crown Him Lord of all.

Sinners, whose love can ne'er forget the wormwood and the gall,
Go spread your trophies at His feet, and crown Him Lord of all.
Go spread your trophies at His feet, and crown Him Lord of all.

Let every tribe and every tongue before Him prostrate fall
And shout in universal song the crownéd Lord of all.
And shout in universal song the crownèd Lord of all.

Santa Claus

CAN SANTA CLAUS BE SAVED?

The angel answered, "The Holy Spirit will come upon you,
and the power of the Most High will overshadow you.
So the holy one to be born will be called the Son of God."

—LUKE 1:35

Believe it or not, even Santa can be saved! Far from being a dangerous fairy tale, *Santa Claus* in reality is an Anglicized form of the Dutch name *Sinter Klaas*, which in turn is a reference to Saint Nicholas, a Christian bishop from the fourth century. According to tradition, Saint Nick not only lavished gifts on needy children, but also valiantly supported the doctrine of the Trinity at the Council of Nicea in AD 325.[4] While the word *Trinity*—like *incarnation*—is not found in Scripture, it aptly codifies what God has condescended to reveal to us about His nature and being. The Trinitarian platform contains three planks.

The first plank underscores the reality that there is but one God.

Christianity is not polytheistic, but fiercely monotheistic. "'You are my witnesses,' declares the LORD, 'and my servant whom I have chosen, so that you may know and believe me and understand that I am he. *Before me no god was formed, nor will there be one after me*'" (Isaiah 43:10; emphasis added).

The second plank emphasizes that in hundreds of Scripture passages, the Father, the Son, and the Holy Spirit are declared to be fully and completely God. As a case in point, the apostle Paul says that "there is but one God, the Father" (1 Corinthians 8:6). The Father, speaking of the Son, says, "Your throne, O God, will last for ever and ever" (Hebrews 1:8). And when Ananias "lied to the Holy Spirit," Peter points out that he had "not lied to men but to God" (Acts 5:3–4).

The third plank of the Trinitarian platform asserts that the Father, Son, and Holy Spirit are eternally distinct. Scripture clearly portrays subject/object relationships between Father, Son, and Holy Spirit. For example, the Father and Son love each other (John 5:20; 14:31), speak to each other (John 17:1–26), and together send the Holy Spirit (John 15:26). Additionally, Jesus proclaims that He and the Father are two distinct witnesses and two distinct judges (John 8:14–18). If Jesus were Himself the Father, His argument would not only have been irrelevant, it would have been fatally flawed; and, if such were the case, He could not have been fully God. It is important to note that when Trinitarians speak of one *God*, they are referring to the nature or essence of God. Moreover, when they speak of *persons*, they are referring to personal self-distinctions within the Godhead. Put another way, we believe in one *What* and three *Who's*.

In sum, then, Christians may look back to the tradition of Saint Nick, who lavished gifts on the needy and valiantly supported the doctrine of the Trinity at the Council of Nicea, as a legendary hero of the faith. Of course, the notion that Santa Claus lives at the North Pole in a toy factory, that he sees children at all times and knows whether they've been bad or good, and that he travels in a sled pulled by flying reindeer, is clearly myth and should therefore be treated as such.

This December 25 as you celebrate the coming of Christ with a Christmas tree surrounded by presents, may the story of selflessness on the part of Saint Nick remind you of the Savior who gave the greatest gift of all. Thus, rather than supplant the Savior with Santa, we can use Saint Nick as a reminder to generously support God-ordained ministries so that the message of salvation can reach those who have not as yet received salvation by God's grace alone, through faith alone—and on account of Christ alone.

In the sixth month, God sent the angel Gabriel to Nazareth, a town in Galilee, to a virgin pledged to be married to a man named Joseph, a descendant of David. The virgin's name was Mary. The angel went to her and said, "Greetings, you who are highly favored! The Lord is with you."

Mary was greatly troubled at his words and wondered what kind of greeting this might be. But the angel said to her, "Do not be afraid, Mary, you have found favor with God. You will be with child and give birth to a son, and you are to give him the name Jesus. He will be great and will be called the Son of the Most High. The Lord God will give him the throne of his father David, and he will reign over the house of Jacob forever; his kingdom will never end."

"How will this be," Mary asked the angel, "since I am a virgin?"

The angel answered, "The Holy Spirit will come upon you, and the power of the Most High will overshadow you. So the holy one to be born will be called the Son of God." (Luke 1:26–35)

QUESTIONS

+ Where did the "Santa Claus" tradition originate?
+ What are the three planks of the Trinitarian platform?

HOLY, HOLY, HOLY!
Reginald Heber

Holy, holy, holy! Lord God Almighty!
Early in the morning our song shall rise to Thee;
Holy, holy, holy! merciful and mighty!
God in three Persons, blessed Trinity.

Holy, holy, holy! all the saints adore Thee,
Casting down their golden crowns around the crystal sea;
Cherubim and seraphim falling down before Thee,
Who wast, and art, and evermore shalt be.

Holy, holy, holy! though the darkness hide Thee,
Though the eye of sinful man Thy glory may not see;
Only Thou art holy! There is none beside Thee,
Perfect in power, in love, and purity.

Holy, holy, holy! Lord God Almighty!
All Thy works shall praise Thy Name, in earth, and sky, and sea;
Holy, holy, holy! merciful and mighty!
God in three Persons, blessed Trinity!

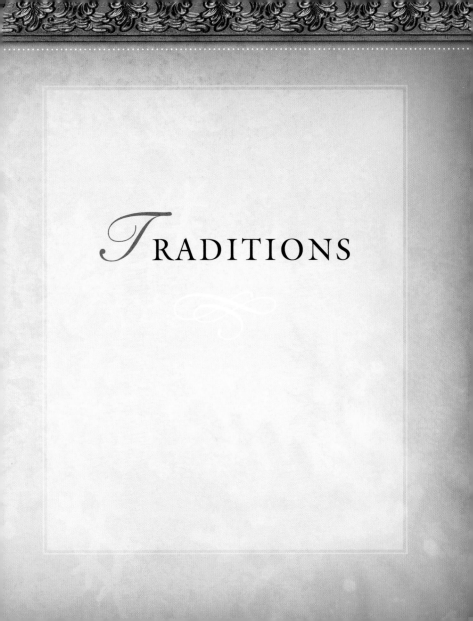

TRADITIONS

THE CHRISTMAS TREE TRADITION

To him who overcomes, I will give the right to eat from the tree of life,
which is in the paradise of God.

—REVELATION 2:7B

This Christmas season, as in those gone by, it is commonplace to hear Christians condemn trees adorned with ornaments as idolatrous. The following passage from Jeremiah is often cited as support for the condemnation:

This is what the LORD says:

"Do not learn the ways of the nations
or be terrified by signs in the sky,
though the nations are terrified by them.
For the customs of the peoples are worthless;
they cut a tree out of the forest,

> *and a craftsman shapes it with his chisel. They adorn it with silver*
>> *and gold;*
> *they fasten it with hammer and nails*
> *so that it will not totter*" (Jeremiah 10:2–4, emphasis added).

While this passage may sound to modern ears like an uncanny description of Christmas trees from the sixth century BC, the historical and biblical context precludes this anachronistic reading of the text. The very next verse precludes the pretext: "'Like a scarecrow in a melon patch, their *idols* cannot speak; they must be carried because they cannot walk'" (Jeremiah 10:5, emphasis added). Jeremiah's description of a tree cut out of the forest and adorned with silver and gold and fastened with a hammer and nails so that it would not totter is, therefore, a reference to *wooden idols*, not *Christmas trees*.

In point of fact, Christmas trees originated in Christian Germany two thousand years after Jeremiah's condemnation of manmade idols. They evolved over time from two Christian traditions. One was a "paradise tree" hung with apples as a reminder of the tree of life in the Garden of Eden. The other was a triangular shelf holding Christmas figurines decorated by a star. In the sixteenth century, these two symbols merged into the present Christmas tree tradition.[5]

As such, the Christmas tree began as a distinctively Christian symbol and can still be legitimately used by Christians today as part of their Christmas festivities. Christmas trees are not, however, essential to Christmas. Christian celebrations can certainly be complete without a tree adorned with ornaments. Like all symbolic objects that aid worshipful remembrance and celebration of Christ (e.g., the elements of communion, baptismal water, crosses, paintings, and so forth), we must never allow Christmas trees to take the place of that to which they point: namely, God's eternal redemptive purposes from the fall in Paradise to salvation in Christ.

It is my prayer that this Christmas season you will be reminded to use the symbolism of the Christmas tree in the home of an unbeliever as an opportunity to explain that the reason for the season is the Savior.

READING

"Behold, I will create
    new heavens and a new earth.
The former things will not be remembered,
    nor will they come to mind.
But be glad and rejoice forever
    in what I will create,
for I will create Jerusalem to be a delight

and its people a joy.
I will rejoice over Jerusalem
     and take delight in my people;
the sound of weeping and of crying
     will be heard in it no more.

"Never again will there be in it
     an infant who lives but a few days,
     or an old man who does not live out his years;
he who dies at a hundred
     will be thought a mere youth;
he who fails to reach a hundred
     will be considered accursed.
 They will build houses and dwell in them;
     they will plant vineyards and eat their fruit.
No longer will they build houses and others live in them,
     or plant and others eat.
For as the days of a tree,
     so will be the days of my people;
my chosen ones will long enjoy
     the works of their hands.
 They will not toil in vain
     or bear children doomed to misfortune;

for they will be a people blessed by the LORD,
>   they and their descendants with them.
Before they call I will answer;
>   while they are still speaking I will hear.
The wolf and the lamb will feed together,
>   and the lion will eat straw like the ox,
>   but dust will be the serpent's food.
They will neither harm nor destroy
>   on all my holy mountain,"
says the LORD. (Isaiah 65:17–25)

QUESTIONS

+ What is the real meaning of Jeremiah 10:2–5?
+ What is the real origin of the Christmas tree tradition?

Joyful, Joyful We Adore Thee
Henry van Dyke

Joyful, joyful, we adore Thee,
God of glory, Lord of love:
Hearts unfold like flowers before Thee,
Opening to the sun above.
Melt the clouds of sin and sadness;
Drive the dark of doubt away;
Giver of immortal gladness,
Fill us with the light of day!

All Thy works with joy surround Thee,
Earth and heaven reflect Thy rays,
Stars and angels sing around Thee,
Center of unbroken praise.
Field and forest, vale and mountain,
Flowery meadow, flashing sea,
Singing bird and flowing fountain,
Call us to rejoice in Thee.

Thou art giving and forgiving,
Ever blessing, ever blest,

Wellspring of the joy of living,
Ocean-depth of happy rest!
Thou our Father, Christ our Brother,
All who live in love are Thine;
Teach us how to love each other,
Lift us to the joy divine.

ARE IMAGES IDOLATROUS?

The Son is the radiance of God's glory and the exact representation
of his being, sustaining all things by his powerful word. After he had provided
purification for sins, he sat down at the right hand of the Majesty in heaven.

—HEBREWS 1:3

It is not at all uncommon to see images such as Caravaggio's *Madonna and Child* or Da Vinci's *Virgin and Child* in magazines, in movies, or in manuscripts. Which begs the question: Are such images of Jesus idolatrous? Byzantine Emperor Leo III apparently thought so. As such, in the fourth century AD he ordered the abolition of icons (revered images or sculptures) of Jesus, Mary, angels, and saints. This sparked the great Iconoclastic Controversy, so called because those who supported the eradication of icons, often on the grounds that they violated the second commandment's prohibition of graven images, were known as iconoclasts or "image breakers." The controversy sparked in the fourth century persists to this very day. As such, the question emerges "Do the images of Jesus really violate the second commandment?"

To begin with, if the second commandment condemns images of Jesus, then it condemns making images of anything at all. Therefore, God would have been guilty of contradiction Himself because He commanded the Israelites to adorn the Ark of the Covenant with the images of cherubim (Exodus 25:18–20).

Furthermore, in context, the commandment is not an injunction against making "graven images," but an injunction against worshiping them. As such, God warns, "You shall not make for yourself an idol in the form of anything in heaven above or on the earth beneath or in the waters below. *You shall not bow down to them or worship them*; for I, the LORD your God, am a jealous God" (Exodus 20:4–5, emphasis added).

Finally, if viewing an image necessarily leads to idolatry, then the incarnation of Christ was the greatest temptation of all. Yet Jesus thought it appropriate for people to look on Him and worship Him as God (Matthew 28:9; Luke 24:52). That worship, however, was to be directed to His person, not to His appearance. Indeed, idolatry lies not in the making of images, but in the worship of man-made images in the place of the "image of the invisible God" (Colossians 1:15).

This Christmas season, may images of Jesus, Mary, old Saint

Nick, and angels praising God on high cause you to worship the incarnate God saying, "Glory to God in the highest, and on earth peace to men on whom his favor rests" (Luke 2:14).

READING

In the past God spoke to our forefathers through the prophets at many times and in various ways, but in these last days he has spoken to us by his Son, whom he appointed heir of all things, and through whom he made the universe. The Son is the radiance of God's glory and the exact representation of his being, sustaining all things by his powerful word. After he had provided purification for sins, he sat down at the right hand of the Majesty in heaven. So he became as much superior to the angels as the name he has inherited is superior to theirs.

For to which of the angels did God ever say,

> "You are my Son;
> today I have become your Father"?

Or again,

> "I will be his Father,
> and he will be my Son"?

And again, when God brings his firstborn into the world, he says,

> "Let all God's angels worship him."

In speaking of the angels he says,

> "He makes his angels winds,
> his servants flames of fire."

But about the Son he says,

> "Your throne, O God, will last for ever and ever,
> and righteousness will be the scepter of your kingdom.
> You have loved righteousness and hated wickedness;
> therefore God, your God, has set you above your companions
> by anointing you with the oil of joy."

He also says,

> "In the beginning, O Lord, you laid the foundations of the earth,
> and the heavens are the work of your hands.
> They will perish, but you remain;
> they will all wear out like a garment.
> You will roll them up like a robe;
> like a garment they will be changed.
> But you remain the same,
> and your years will never end."

To which of the angels did God ever say,

> "Sit at my right hand

until I make your enemies

a footstool for your feet"?

Are not all angels ministering spirits sent to serve those who will inherit salvation? (Hebrews 1:1–14)

QUESTIONS

+ Why did early Christians seek to rid the church of icons or images?

+ In what ways can Christmas art (e.g., nativity scenes, paintings, ornaments, etc.) enhance our worship of Christ?

GOOD CHRISTIAN MEN, REJOICE

Heinrich Suso; English Translation by John M. Neale

Good Christian men, rejoice
With heart and soul and voice;
Give ye heed to what we say:
News! News!
Jesus Christ is born today!
Ox and ass before Him bow,
And He is in the manger now.
Christ is born today!
Christ is born today!

Good Christian men, rejoice
With heart and soul and voice;
Now ye hear of endless bliss:
Joy! Joy!
Jesus Christ was born for this!
He hath opened the heav'nly door,
And man is blessed evermore.
Christ was born for this!
Christ was born for this!

Good Christian men, rejoice
With heart and soul and voice;
Now ye need not fear the grave:
Peace! Peace!
Jesus Christ was born to save!
Calls you one and calls you all
To gain His everlasting hall.
Christ was born to save!
Christ was born to save!

THE MAGI

*"Where is the one who has been born
king of the Jews? We saw his star in the east
and have come to worship him."*

—MATTHEW 2:2

No single tradition is more widely adhered to during the Christmas season than that of giving gifts. This tradition is firmly rooted in the biblical account of the Magi who saw a star in the east and came to worship Jesus. "On coming to the house, they saw the child with his mother Mary, and they bowed down and worshiped him. Then they opened their treasures and presented him with gifts of gold and of incense and of myrrh" (Matthew 2:11).

Despite its biblical basis, gift giving has been vigorously challenged by followers of Herbert W. Armstrong as well as by organizations such as the Watchtower Society. Their basic argument is that *Magi* means "astrologers" and that God would never lead His people to give gifts at Christmas on the basis of astrology.

In response it should first be noted that even if the Magi did practice astrology, the Bible makes it crystal clear that the wise men were *led by God* both by means of the star, which guided them to Christ (Matthew 2:9), and by means of the warning that kept them from returning to Herod (Matthew 2:12). Furthermore, contrary to the practice of astrology, which involves divination and attempts to predict the future apart from God, the star the Magi followed was not used to *foretell* the future, but to *forth tell* the future. In other words, the star of Bethlehem did not *prophesy* the birth of Christ; it *pronounced* the birth of Christ.

Finally, it is interesting to note that, contrary to popular tradition, the Magi were not necessarily three kings. While Matthew's gospel narrative does teach that wise men visited Jesus and His parents shortly after His birth, Matthew never specifies how many wise men there were. The traditional belief that there were three wise men originated from the fact that they brought gifts of gold, frankincense, and myrrh (Matthew 2:11). Consequently, while the biblical account is consistent with the possibility of three wise men, there is no strong biblical or extra-biblical evidence in support of this numbering. Neither is there any biblical support for the naming of the Magi. Tradition beginning sometime in the sixth century named the wise men Melkon (or Melchior), Balthazar, and Gaspar.[6] As with the numbering of the Magi, these names should be attributed to folklore and tradition rather than to historical fact.

On the one hand, the exchanging of gifts can be dangerous in that gift giving has a powerful potential for promoting crass materialism. On the other, the giving of gifts reinforces the reality that "it is more blessed to give than to receive" (Acts 20:35). This Christmas season, may we be ever more mindful that the greatest gift we can give to another human being is the Christ Child. When He enters the human heart, everlasting life becomes a present reality.

READING

After Jesus was born in Bethlehem in Judea, during the time of King Herod, Magi from the east came to Jerusalem and asked, "Where is the one who has been born king of the Jews? We saw his star in the east and have come to worship him."

When King Herod heard this he was disturbed, and all Jerusalem with him. When he had called together all the people's chief priests and teachers of the law, he asked them where the Christ was to be born. "In Bethlehem in Judea," they replied, "for this is what the prophet has written:

"'But you, Bethlehem, in the land of Judah,
    are by no means least among the rulers of Judah;
for out of you will come a ruler
    who will be the shepherd of my people Israel.'"

Then Herod called the Magi secretly and found out from them the exact time the star had appeared. He sent them to Bethlehem and said, "Go and make a careful search for the child. As soon as you find him, report to me, so that I too may go and worship him."

After they had heard the king, they went on their way, and the star they had seen in the east went ahead of them until it stopped over the place where the child was. When they saw the star, they were overjoyed. On coming to the house, they saw the child with his mother Mary, and they bowed down and worshiped him. Then they opened their treasures and presented him with gifts of gold and of incense and of myrrh. And having been warned in a dream not to go back to Herod, they returned to their country by another route. (Matthew 2:1–12)

QUESTIONS

+ How did the tradition of three wise men come into being?
+ What are pros and cons to the giving of gifts?

WE THREE KINGS OF ORIENT ARE

Rev. Henry Hopkins, Jr.

We three kings of Orient are;
Bearing gifts we traverse afar,
Field and fountain, moor and mountain—
Following yonder star.
O star of wonder, star of night,
Star with royal beauty bright,
Westward leading, still proceeding,
Guide us to thy perfect light.

Born a King on Bethlehem's plain:
Gold I bring to crown him again,
King forever, ceasing never,
Over us all to reign.
O star of wonder, star of night,
Star with royal beauty bright,
Westward leading, still proceeding,
Guide us to thy perfect light.

Frankincense to offer have I;
Incense owns a Deity nigh;

Prayer and praising, voices raising;
Worshiping God on high.
O star of wonder, star of night,
Star with royal beauty bright,
Westward leading, still proceeding,
Guide us to thy perfect light.

Myrrh is mine, its bitter perfume
Breathes a life of gathering gloom;
Sorrowing, sighing, bleeding, dying,
Sealed in the stone-cold tomb.
O star of wonder, star of night,
Star with royal beauty bright,
Westward leading, still proceeding,
Guide us to thy perfect light.

Glorious now behold Him arise;
King and God and sacrifice;
Alleluia, Alleluia,
Sounds through the earth and skies.
O star of wonder, star of night,
Star with royal beauty bright,
Westward leading, still proceeding,
Guide us to thy perfect light.

Day 18

EPIPHANY

After Jesus was born in Bethlehem in Judea, during the time of
King Herod, Magi from the east came to Jerusalem.

—MATTHEW 2:1

piphany (meaning "to reveal") is arguably the oldest and most significant of all the Christmas traditions. It highlights the reality that due to our sin we cannot come to God; thus, God in Christ *revealed* Himself to us. The tradition of Epiphany, also known as "Three Kings Day" (*Driekoningendag*), is celebrated January 6 as recognition of the first Gentiles to acknowledge Jesus as King. As such it corresponds to Simeon's exultation, "For my eyes have seen your salvation, which you have prepared in the sight of all people, *a light for revelation to the Gentiles*" (Luke 2: 30–32; emphasis added).

While Epiphany provides an extraordinarily meaningful climax to the Christmas season, it is ultimately rooted in tradition. The text of Matthew 2:11 notes that at the time of visitation by the wise men, Mary and Joseph were no longer in the place of Jesus' birth, which contained a manger. Rather, they were now in "a house." Moreover, the meagerness of Mary's purification offering (Luke 2:22–24; cf. Leviticus 12:2–8) suggests that forty days after the birth of Christ, the day of the offering, Joseph and his family were still living in relative poverty. According to the Levitical law, Mary's offering—"two doves or two young pigeons"—was the prescribed purification offering for one who had become unclean through childbirth and could not afford to offer a lamb (Leviticus 12:8). Had the wise men already arrived at the time of Mary's purification offering, their generous gifts might well have made it possible for Mary to afford a lamb, as recommended in the Levitical law. In short, while Scripture does not indicate the exact date of the visit of the wise men, there is reason to believe that the visitors from the East did not arrive until some time after the day of Mary's purification offering, which took place forty days after the birth of Jesus.

While it is important to separate truth from traditions, we must never cease to emulate the reverence and worship for the King of kings and Lord of lords manifested by the wise men. As such, when entities suggest that the wise men gave gifts to Christ, not to one another, we should immediately recognize that they have missed the point entirely. As Scripture makes abundantly clear, giving *to others* (particularly those in need) is tantamount to giving *to Christ* (Matthew 25:31–46). On Day 18 of your trek toward the heart of Christmas, may the Epiphany tradition encourage you to use your time, talent, and treasure to make the King of kings and Lord of lords known to the nations.

READING

On the eighth day, when it was time to circumcise him, he was named Jesus, the name the angel had given him before he had been conceived.

When the time of their purification according to the Law of Moses had been completed, Joseph and Mary took him to Jerusalem to present him to the Lord (as it is written in the Law of the Lord, "Every firstborn male is to be consecrated to the Lord"), and to offer a sacrifice in keeping with what is said in the Law of the Lord: "a pair of doves or two young pigeons."

Now there was a man in Jerusalem called Simeon, who was righteous and devout. He was waiting for the consolation of Israel, and the Holy Spirit was upon him. It had been revealed to him by the Holy Spirit that he would not die before he had seen the Lord's Christ. Moved by the Spirit, he went into the temple courts. When the parents brought in the child Jesus to do for him what the custom of the Law required, Simeon took him in his arms and praised God, saying:

"Sovereign Lord, as you have promised,
　　you now dismiss your servant in peace.
For my eyes have seen your salvation,
　　which you have prepared in the sight of all people,
a light for revelation to the Gentiles
　　and for glory to your people Israel." (Luke 2:21–32)

--- QUESTIONS ---

+ What is the meaning of the word *Epiphany*?
+ Why is the story of the wise men significant to us today?

THE FIRST NOEL
Traditional English Carol

The first Noel, the angel did say,
Was to certain poor shepherds in fields as they lay;
In fields where they lay keeping their sheep,
On a cold winter's night that was so deep.
Noel, Noel, Noel, Noel,
Born is the King of Israel.

They looked up and saw a star
Shining in the east, beyond them far,
And to the earth it gave great light,
And so it continued both day and night.
Noel, Noel, Noel, Noel,
Born is the King of Israel.

And by the light of that same star
Three wise men came from country far;
To seek for a king was their intent,
And to follow the star wherever it went.
Noel, Noel, Noel, Noel,
Born is the King of Israel.

Then let us all with one accord
Sing praises to our heavenly Lord;
Who hath made heaven and earth of naught,
And with His blood mankind hath bought.
Noel, Noel, Noel, Noel,
Born is the King of Israel.

Day 19

THE GIVING OF GIFTS

*Just as you excel in everything—in faith, in speech, in knowledge,
in complete earnestness and in your love for us—see that you
also excel in this grace of giving.*

—2 CORINTHIANS 8:7

Some of the most troublesome aspects of gift giving are the materialism and commercialism that are so inextricably woven into the fabric of Christmas and the attendant pressure of giving gifts to others out of a sense of obligation, rather than freely out of love.

While we can all identify with such pressure, it is important to recognize that perversions do not in and of themselves invalidate the practice of giving gifts. As followers of the One who gave Himself for us, we ought to exult in the very notion of giving to others. As such, having the unique opportunity of giving to ministries that propagate the gospel, of giving to the downtrodden and oft-forgotten, and of giving to family members and friends should overwhelm us with joy—especially when there is no expectation of giving to get. Jesus' teachings in this regard are instructive.

While dining at the house of a prominent Pharisee, Jesus admonished the guests (and presumably the host as well), saying:

> When you give a luncheon or dinner, do not invite your friends, your brothers or relatives, or your rich neighbors; if you do, they may invite you back and so you will be repaid. But when you give a banquet, invite the poor, the crippled, the lame, the blind, and you will be blessed. Although they cannot repay you, you will be repaid at the resurrection of the righteous (Luke 14:12–14).

Far from suggesting that it is inappropriate to show kindness and generosity to family and friends, Jesus highlights the reality of *genuine* kindness and generosity motivated by love for others as opposed to the expectation of favor in return.

This Christmas season may we give with a grateful heart, as we too have been given. Far from a burden, giving can become an extraordinary blessing. As such, whether you are inscribing a Christmas card or purchasing a gift for a loved one, do it all with a grateful heart and a song upon your lips. And "when you give to the needy," remember the words of the greatest Gift of all: "Do not let your left hand know what your right hand is doing, so that your giving may be in secret. Then your Father, who sees what is done in secret, will reward you" (Matthew 6:3-4).

This is how we know what love is: Jesus Christ laid down his life for us. And we ought to lay down our lives for our brothers. If anyone has material possessions and sees his brother in need but has no pity on him, how can the love of God be in him? Dear children, let us not love with words or tongue but with actions and in truth. This then is how we know that we belong to the truth, and how we set our hearts at rest in his presence whenever our hearts condemn us. For God is greater than our hearts, and he knows everything. (1 John 3:16-20)

→ ——————————————| QUESTIONS |—————————————— ←

+ How does Christmas afford a unique opportunity to learn the art of selfless giving?
+ What are the inherent dangers of giving to get?

TAKE MY LIFE
Frances R. Havergal

Take my life, and let it be consecrated, Lord, to Thee.
Take my moments and my days; let them flow in ceaseless praise.
Take my hands, and let them move at the impulse of Thy love.
Take my feet, and let them be swift and beautiful for Thee.

Take my voice, and let me sing always, only, for my King.
Take my lips, and let them be filled with messages from Thee.
Take my silver and my gold; not a mite would I withhold.
Take my intellect, and use every power as Thou shalt choose.

Take my will, and make it Thine; it shall be no longer mine.
Take my heart, it is Thine own; it shall be Thy royal throne.
Take my love, my Lord, I pour at Thy feet its treasure store.
Take myself, and I will be ever, only, all for Thee.

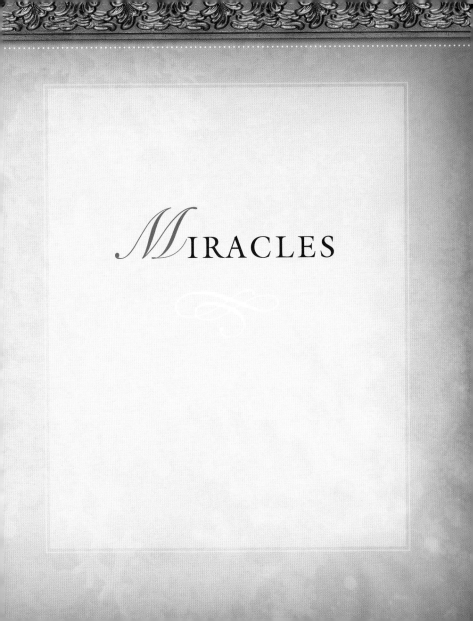

MIRACLES

MIRACLE OR MYTH?

Many have undertaken to draw up an account of the things that have been fulfilled among us, just as they were handed down to us by those who from the first were eyewitnesses and servants of the word. Therefore, since I myself have carefully investigated everything from the beginning, it seemed good also to me to write an orderly account for you, most excellent Theophilus, so that you may know the certainty of the things you have been taught.

—LUKE 1:1–4

odernity has left many with the false impression that the virgin birth is nothing more than ancient superstition. In an op-ed piece published by the *New York Times*, columnist Nicholas Kristof used the virgin birth of Jesus to shamelessly promote the Enlightenment's false dichotomy between faith and reason. In his words, "The faith in the Virgin Birth reflects the way American Christianity is becoming less intellectual and more mystical over time." Kristof ends his piece with the following patronizing comment: "The heart is a wonderful organ, but so is the brain." Those who have a truly open mind, however, should resist rejecting the virgin birth *a priori* (prior to examination).[7]

First, miracles are not only possible, but they are necessary in order to make sense of the universe in which we live. According to modern science, the universe not only had a beginning, but it is unfathomably fine-tuned to support life. Not only so, but the origin of life, information in the genetic code, irreducible complexity of biological systems, and the phenomenon of the human mind pose intractable difficulties for merely natural explanations. Thus, reason forces us to look beyond the natural world to a supernatural Designer who periodically intervenes in the affairs of His created handiwork. In other words, if we are willing to believe that God created the heavens and the earth (Genesis 1:1), we should have no problem accepting the virgin birth.

Furthermore, we are compelled by reason and evidence to acknowledge that the Bible is divine rather than merely human in origin (see Day 5, on pages 25–29). The miraculous preservation of God's Word via manuscripts, archaeology, and prophecy together provide a cumulative case for the reliability of Scripture. Thus, we may legitimately appeal to the Word of God as supernatural evidence for the virgin birth. Moreover, Christ, who demonstrated that He was God in human flesh through the supernatural fact of His resurrection, pronounced the Scriptures infallible (John 10:35; 14:24–26; 15:26–27; 16:13; Hebrews 1:1–2). And if Christ concurs with the biblical record of the virgin birth, no one should have the temerity to contradict His claim.

Finally, while it is currently popular to suggest that the gospel writers borrowed the virgin birth motif from pagan mythology, the facts say otherwise. Stories of gods having sexual intercourse with women—such as the sun god Apollo becoming a snake and impregnating the mother of Augustus Caesar—hardly parallel the virgin birth account. What is more, given the strict monotheistic worldview of New Testament authors, it should stretch credulity beyond the breaking point to suppose they borrowed from pagan mythologies—especially myths extolling the sexual exploits of pagan gods!

As we encounter those who capriciously cast aspersions on the miraculous nature of the virgin birth, we would do well to remember that it is our responsibility to use our well-reasoned responses as springboards for demonstrating that the historical account of Christ's coming in flesh is faith founded on irrefutable fact.

In the sixth month, God sent the angel Gabriel to Nazareth, a town in Galilee, to a virgin pledged to be married to a man named Joseph, a descendant of David. The virgin's name was Mary. The angel went to her and said, "Greetings, you who are highly favored! The Lord is with you."

Mary was greatly troubled at his words and wondered what kind of greeting this might be. But the angel said to her, "Do not be afraid, Mary, you have found favor with God. You will be with child and give birth to a son, and you are to give him the name Jesus. He will be great and will be called the Son of the Most High. The Lord God will give him the throne of his father David, and he will reign over the house of Jacob forever; his kingdom will never end."

"How will this be," Mary asked the angel, "since I am a virgin?"

The angel answered, "The Holy Spirit will come upon you, and the power of the Most High will overshadow you. So the holy one to be born will be called the Son of God. Even Elizabeth your relative is going to have a child in her old age, and she who was said to be barren is in her sixth month. For nothing is impossible with God."

"I am the Lord's servant," Mary answered. "May it be to me as you have said." Then the angel left her. (Luke 1:26–38)

+ Why should we allow for both natural and supernatural explanations in order to make sense of the world in which we live?

+ Why isn't appealing to Scripture as the basis for believing in the miraculous virgin birth merely circular reasoning?

HARK! THE HERALD ANGELS SING

Charles Wesley

Hark! The herald angels sing, "Glory to the newborn King!
Peace on earth and mercy mild, God and sinners reconciled!"
Joyful all ye nations rise; join the triumph of the skies;
With th' angelic host proclaim, "Christ is born in Bethlehem!"
Hark! The herald angels sing, "Glory to the newborn King!"

Christ, by highest heaven adored, Christ, the everlasting Lord:
Late in time, behold him come; offspring of a virgin's womb.
Veiled in flesh the Godhead see; hail th' incarnate Deity,
Pleased as man with men to dwell, Jesus, our Emmanuel!
Hark! The herald angels sing, "Glory to the newborn King!"

Hail the heaven-born Prince of Peace! Hail the Son of Righteousness!
Light and life to all he brings, risen with healing in his wings.
Mild, he lays his glory by, born that man no more may die;
Born to raise the sons of earth, born to give them second birth.
Hark! The herald angels sing, "Glory to the newborn King!"

ADVENT

THE FIRST ADVENT

For to us a child is born, to us a son is given,
and the government will be on his shoulders.
And he will be called Wonderful Counselor, Mighty God,
Everlasting Father, Prince of Peace.

—ISAIAH 9:6

The term *Advent* (from the Latin, *Adventus*) literally means "coming." As such, Advent is a season in which the Christian church celebrates the *coming* in flesh of our Lord and Savior Jesus Christ. The Advent Church calendar is rife with traditions from biblical readings to the successive lighting of candles on an Advent wreath.

The glory of Advent finds its genesis in Old Testament prophecies that point forward to the coming incarnation of Christ. Moses' prophecy that God would raise up a prophet like him from among the Israelites (Deuteronomy 18:15) typologically points forward to *the* Prophet, Jesus Christ. Within the context of the Old Testament, the prophecy that God would raise up another prophet like Moses was fulfilled in the fore-future in Joshua, who led the children of Israel into the Promised Land (see Deuteronomy 31). In addition to its near-future fulfillment in Joshua, this prophecy came to be understood as pointing forward to an eschatological prophet who would lead the people of God as a new Moses and a new Joshua. As Joshua (meaning "salvation") led the children of Israel into the land of promise, so Jesus will lead His people into "the new Jerusalem, coming down out of heaven from God" (Revelation 21:2).

The Gospel of John reveals that this hope was alive and well in the first century AD (cf. John 1:21; 6:14; 7:40), and Stephen implicitly identifies Jesus as the ultimate fulfillment of this prophecy in the impassioned sermon for which he was martyred (Acts 7:37–38). In this way, both Moses' prophecy and its near-future fulfillment in Joshua serve as types of the great Prophet of God who not only spoke the words of God but was Himself the Word become flesh (John 1:14; cf. Hebrews 1:1–2).

The beauty of the gospel is that Abraham (the father of many nations) was promised a royal seed—and that seed is Christ. However, as the apostle Paul explains, all who are clothed in Christ constitute one congruent chosen covenant community connected by the cross. "If you belong to Christ, then you are Abraham's seed, and heirs according to the promise" (Galatians 3:29). The "mystery" is this, says Paul, "that through the gospel the Gentiles are heirs together with Israel, members together of one body, and sharers together in the promise in Christ Jesus" (Ephesians 3:6).

This is how the birth of Jesus Christ came about: His mother Mary was pledged to be married to Joseph, but before they came together, she was found to be with child through the Holy Spirit. Because Joseph her husband was a righteous man and did not want to expose her to public disgrace, he had in mind to divorce her quietly.

But after he had considered this, an angel of the Lord appeared to him in a dream and said, "Joseph son of David, do not be afraid to take Mary home as your wife, because what is conceived in her is from the Holy Spirit. She will give birth to a son, and you are to give him the name Jesus, because he will save his people from their sins."

All this took place to fulfill what the Lord had said through the prophet: "The virgin will be with child and will give birth to a son, and they will call him Immanuel"—which means, "God with us."

When Joseph woke up, he did what the angel of the Lord had commanded him and took Mary home as his wife. But he had no union with her until she gave birth to a son. And he gave him the name Jesus. (Matthew 1:18–25)

QUESTIONS

+ What does the term *advent* mean?
+ How did Joshua foreshadow Jesus?

O HOLY NIGHT

John S. Dwight, based upon a French poem by
Placide Cappeau de Roquemaure

O Holy Night! the stars are brightly shining,
It is the night of the dear Savior's birth!
Long lay the world in sin and error pining,
Till He appeared and the soul felt its worth.
A thrill of hope the weary world rejoices,
For yonder breaks a new and glorious morn.
Fall on your knees! Oh, hear the angel voices!
O night divine, O night when Christ was born!
O night, O holy night, O night divine!

Led by the light of faith serenely beaming,
With glowing hearts by His cradle we stand;
So led by the light of a star sweetly gleaming,
Here came the wise men from Orient land.
The King of kings lay thus in lowly manger,
In all our trials born to be our Friend;
He knows our need, to our weakness is no stranger.
Behold your King! Before Him lowly bend!
Behold your King! Before Him lowly bend!

Truly He taught us to love one another;
His law is love and His gospel is peace.
Chains shall He break, for the slave is our brother,
And in His name all oppression shall cease.
Sweet hymns of joy in grateful chorus raise we,
Let all within us praise His holy name;
Christ is the Lord, O, praise His name forever!
His power and glory evermore proclaim!
His power and glory evermore proclaim!

THE DAILY ADVENT OF CHRIST

Every day they continued to meet together in the temple courts.
They broke bread in their homes and ate together with glad and sincere
hearts, praising God and enjoying the favor of all the people. And the
Lord added to their number daily those who were being saved.

—ACTS 2:46–47

Yesterday we concentrated on the First Advent of Christ. But there's more. The celebration of the coming of Christ in flesh is an everyday reality. As such, we celebrate the daily advent of Christ through prayer, praise, and proclamation of the Word made flesh. In prayer, we have the privilege of expressing thanksgiving to the One who saved us, sanctifies us, and one day will glorify us. In praise—not just during Advent, but throughout the year—we express the essence of our faith in "psalms, hymns and spiritual songs" (Ephesians 5:19). And in proclamation we "correct, rebuke and encourage—with great patience and careful instruction" (2 Timothy 4:2).

Furthermore, the daily advent of Christ is celebrated through community, confession, and contribution. Community is visible in baptism, which symbolizes our entrance into a body of believers who are one in the One made flesh. In like fashion, holy communion is an expression of our oneness in Christ. As we all partake of the same elements, we partake of that which the elements symbolize—Christ—through whom we are made one. A further expression of our oneness in the Christ of Christmas is our common confession of faith. As with community and confession, we experience oneness in Christ through the contribution of our time, talents, and treasure. The tragedy of modern Christianity is that all too often, when members of the body hurt or have needs, they are left to fill their void and bind their wounds apart from the body of Christ.

Finally, we celebrate the daily advent of our Savior by testifying to *what* we believe, *why* we believe, and in *whom* we have believed. The gospel of Christ should become such a part of our vocabulary that presenting it is second nature. In like fashion, defending the faith is not an option; it should be a basic competency of everyone who takes the sacred name of Christ upon their lips. In addition to being prepared to communicate the *what* and *why* of our faith, we must be empowered to communicate the *who* of our faith. This is especially essential, in that virtually every theological heresy begins with a misconception of the nature of God.

Today, as you look toward the finish line of our twenty-five-day journey to the heart of Christmas, why not ask the Holy Spirit to expand Advent from a Christmas celebration to a daily coming of Christ through worship, through oneness, and through your witness.

✧ ——————————— | READING | ——————————— ✧

Be very careful, then, how you live—not as unwise but as wise, making the most of every opportunity, because the days are evil. Therefore do not be foolish, but understand what the Lord's will is. Do not get drunk on wine, which leads to debauchery. Instead, be filled with the Spirit. Speak to one another with psalms, hymns and spiritual songs. Sing and make music in your heart to the Lord, always giving thanks to God the Father for everything, in the name of our Lord Jesus Christ.

Submit to one another out of reverence for Christ. (Ephesians 5:15–21)

Let us hold unswervingly to the hope we profess, for he who promised is faithful. And let us consider how we may spur one another on toward love and good deeds. Let us not give up meeting together, as some are in the habit of doing, but let us encourage one another—and all the more as you see the Day approaching. (Hebrews 10:23–25)

+ How can you make the advent of Christ an everyday reality in your life?
+ Are you willing to ask the Holy Spirit to expand Advent from a Christmas celebration to a daily experience of the coming of Christ?

ANGELS WE HAVE HEARD ON HIGH
Traditional French Carol (Les Anges dans nos Campagnes),
translated by James Chadwick

Angels we have heard on high, sweetly singing o'er the plains:
And the mountains in reply, echoing their joyous strains.
Gloria in excelsis Deo! Gloria in excelsis Deo!

Shepherds, why this jubilee? Why your joyous strains prolong?
What the gladsome tidings be which inspire your heav'nly song?
Gloria in excelsis Deo! Gloria in excelsis Deo!

Come to Bethlehem and see Him whose birth the angels sing;
Come, adore on bended knee Christ the Lord, the newborn King.
Gloria in excelsis Deo! Gloria in excelsis Deo!

THE FINAL ADVENT OF CHRIST

Now the dwelling of God is with men, and he will live with them.
They will be his people, and God himself will be with them and be their God.
He will wipe every tear from their eyes. There will be no more death or
mourning or crying or pain, for the old order of things has passed away.

—REVELATION 21:3–4

As there is a First Advent and a daily advent, so too there is a final Advent. Just as the focus of the First Advent is Christ coming in flesh, so too the focus of the Second Advent is Christ coming in flesh. This time, however, He will not come as a Babe wrapped in swaddling cloths and lying in a manger; this time He will come as a bridegroom carrying His bride over the threshold of Jordan into the New Jerusalem. As Canaan provided temporal rest for the *physical* descendants of Abraham, the coming Christ will provide eternal rest for His *spiritual* descendants.

In the Final Advent, the land promises that God made to

Abraham will be fully and finally consummated, in that Paradise lost will become Paradise restored. As such, Canaan is typological of a renewed cosmos. Indeed, Abraham, like Isaac and Jacob, viewed living in the Promised Land in much the same way that a stranger would view living in a foreign country. Why? Because as the writer of Hebrews makes plain that, "he was looking forward to the city with foundations, whose architect and builder is God" (Hebrews 11:10). As such, Abraham looked beyond binding borders and boundaries to a day in which the meek would "inherit the earth" (Matthew 5:5; cf. Psalm 37:11, 22).

I don't know about you, but the more I think about the new heaven and the new earth, the more excited I get! It is simply incredible to think that one day soon we will not only experience the resurrection of our carcasses, but we will experience the renewal of the cosmos and the Final Advent of our Creator. We will literally have heaven on earth. Not only will we experience God's fellowship as Adam and Eve did, but we will see the Second Adam face-to-face. God in flesh will live in our midst. And we will never come to the end of exploring the infinite, inexhaustible I AM or the grandeur and glory of His incomparable universe.

Those who die in Christ will experience the new heaven and the new earth as both a physical place in creation and as the personal presence of the Creator:

"The dwelling of God is with men, and he will live with them. They will be his people, and God himself will be with them and be their God. He will wipe every tear from their eyes. There will be no more death or mourning or crying or pain, for the old order of things has passed to.'

He who was seated on the throne said, "I am making everything new!" (Revelation 21:3–5)

This Christmas, as you celebrate the First Advent of our Lord, may His presence in Word and Sacrament sustain you spiritually and may you fix your focus with eager anticipation on the Final Advent of the Babe of Bethlehem—now a Bridegroom returning with His Bride.

READING

A shoot will come up from the stump of Jesse;
    from his roots a Branch will bear fruit.
The Spirit of the LORD will rest on him—
    the Spirit of wisdom and of understanding,
    the Spirit of counsel and of power,
    the Spirit of knowledge and of the fear of the LORD—
and he will delight in the fear of the LORD.

He will not judge by what he sees with his eyes,
    or decide by what he hears with his ears;
but with righteousness he will judge the needy,
    with justice he will give decisions for the poor of the earth.
He will strike the earth with the rod of his mouth;
    with the breath of his lips he will slay the wicked.
Righteousness will be his belt
    and faithfulness the sash around his waist.

The wolf will live with the lamb,
    the leopard will lie down with the goat,
the calf and the lion and the yearling together;
    and a little child will lead them.
The cow will feed with the bear,
    their young will lie down together,
    and the lion will eat straw like the ox.
The infant will play near the hole of the cobra,
    and the young child put his hand into the viper's nest.
They will neither harm nor destroy
    on all my holy mountain,
for the earth will be full of the knowledge of the LORD
    as the waters cover the sea. (Isaiah 11:1–9)

+ What are differences and similarities between the First Advent of Christ and the final one?

+ As Mary and Joseph experienced Jesus face-to-face in the First Advent, so too you will experience the physical presence of Christ in the Second Advent. Focus on seeing Jesus face-to-face. What do you think that will be like?

It Came upon the Midnight Clear
Edmund Sears

It came upon the midnight clear, that glorious song of old,
From angels bending near the earth to touch their harps of gold:
"Peace on the earth, good will to men, from heaven's
all-gracious King!"
The world in solemn stillness lay to hear the angels sing.

Still through the cloven skies they come with
peaceful wings unfurled,
And still their heavenly music floats o'er all the weary world;
Above its sad and lowly plains, they bend on hovering wing,
And ever, o'er its Babel sounds, the blessed angels sing.

Yet with the woes of sin and strife the world hath suffered long;
Beneath the angel-strain have rolled two thousand years of wrong;
And men, at war with men, hear not the love-song which they bring:
O hush the noise, ye men of strife, and hear the angels sing.

For lo! The days are hastening on, by prophet-bards foretold,
When with the ever-circling years shall come the Age of Gold,
When peace shall over all the earth its ancient splendors fling,
And the whole world send back the song which now the angels sing.

$\int$ALVATION

YAHWEH IS SALVATION

She will give birth to a son, and you are to give him the name Jesus,
because he will save his people from their sins.

—MATTHEW 1:21

Hard to believe, but our twenty-five-day odyssey to the heart of Christmas has almost reached its climax. Today, as Christmas Eve approaches, it is time to turn our hearts toward the primary reason for the incarnation of God in Jesus Christ—namely, the salvation of sinners. The very name—Jesus—embodies salvation. *Jesus* is the Greek form of the Hebrew name *Joshua*, meaning "Yahweh saves" or "Yahweh is salvation." Indeed, the Bible is God's unfolding plan of salvation from the fall in Paradise to the promise of Paradise restored.

This Christmas season and throughout the coming year, may you be ever mindful of the reality that God has condescended to use *you* as the means through which the free gift of the water of life is dispensed to a parched and thirsty world. Perhaps you yourself are thirsty! If so, the concluding words of the last book of the Bible have direct application to your life—"Whoever is thirsty, let him come; and whoever wishes, let him take the *free gift* of the water of life" (Revelation 22:17, emphasis added). In essence, there are three steps to this fountain. They are encapsulated in the words *realize*, *repent*, and *receive*.

First, you need to *realize* that you are a sinner. If you do not realize you are a sinner, you will not recognize your need for a savior. The Bible says we "all have sinned and fall short of the glory of God" (Romans 3:23).

Furthermore, you must *repent* of your sins. *Repentance* is an old English word that describes a willingness to turn from our sin toward Jesus Christ. It literally means making a complete U-turn on the road of life—a change of heart and a change of mind. It means that you are willing to follow Jesus and to receive Him as your Savior and Lord. Jesus said, "Repent and believe the good news" (Mark 1:15).

Finally, to demonstrate true belief means to be willing to *receive*. To truly receive is to trust in and depend on Jesus Christ alone to be the Lord of our lives here and now and our Savior for all eternity. It takes more than *knowledge* (the devil knows about Jesus and trembles). It takes more than *agreement* that the knowledge we have is accurate (the devil agrees that Jesus is Lord). What it takes is knowledge, agreement, and *trust* in Jesus Christ alone. The requirements for eternal life are not based on what *you can do*, but on what *Jesus Christ has done*. He stands ready to exchange His perfection for your imperfection.

According to Jesus Christ, those who *realize* they are sinners, *repent* of their sins, and *receive* Him as Savior and Lord are "born again" (John 3:3)—not physically, but spiritually. The reality of our salvation is not dependent on our feelings, but rather on the promise of the Savior who says, "I tell you the truth, whoever hears my word and believes him who sent me has eternal life and will not be condemned; he has crossed over from death to life" (John 5:24).

If you have just confessed your faith in Jesus Christ for the first time, you can rejoice in the angelic proclamation of salvation given to the shepherds on that very first Christmas: "Do not be afraid. I bring you good news of great joy that will be for all the people. Today in the town of David a Savior has been born to you; he is Christ the Lord" (Luke 2:10–11). If, on the other hand, you have already experienced salvation, you have the inestimable privilege of taking the message of salvation to the world.

READING

Who has believed our message
  and to whom has the arm of the Lord been revealed?

He grew up before him like a tender shoot,
>   and like a root out of dry ground.
He had no beauty or majesty to attract us to him,
>   nothing in his appearance that we should desire him.
He was despised and rejected by men,
>   a man of sorrows, and familiar with suffering.
Like one from whom men hide their faces
>   he was despised, and we esteemed him not.
Surely he took up our infirmities
>   and carried our sorrows,
yet we considered him stricken by God,
>   smitten by him, and afflicted.
But he was pierced for our transgressions,
>   he was crushed for our iniquities;
the punishment that brought us peace was upon him,
>   and by his wounds we are healed. (Isaiah 53:1-5)

For God so loved the world that he gave his one and only Son, that whoever believes in him shall not perish but have eternal life. For God did not send his Son into the world to condemn the world, but to save the world through him. Whoever believes in him is not condemned, but whoever does not believe stands condemned already because he has not believed in the name of God's one and only Son.

This is the verdict: Light has come into the world, but men loved darkness instead of light because their deeds were evil. Everyone who does evil hates the light, and will not come into the light for fear that his deeds will be exposed. But whoever lives by the truth comes into the light, so that it may be seen plainly that what he has done has been done through God. (John 3:16–21)

QUESTIONS

+ What are the three steps to the spring of the water of life?
+ What does true belief entail?

SILENT NIGHT
Josef Mohr

Silent night, holy night,
All is calm, all is bright
Round yon virgin mother and child.
Holy Infant so tender and mild,
Sleep in heavenly peace,
Sleep in heavenly peace.

Silent night, holy night.
Shepherds quake at the sight.
Glories stream from heaven afar,
Heavenly hosts sing alleluia;
Christ the Savior is born!
Christ the Savior is born!

Silent night, holy night,
Son of God, love's pure light
Radiant beams from thy holy face,
With the dawn of redeeming grace,
Jesus, Lord, at Thy birth,
Jesus, Lord, at Thy birth!

Silent night, holy night,
Wondrous star, lend thy light.
With the angels let us sing,
"Alleluia" to our King!
Christ the Savior is born,
Christ the Savior is born!

THE SPIRIT OF CHRISTMAS

Now I commit you to God and to the word of his grace, which can build
you up and give you an inheritance among all those who are sanctified.
I have not coveted anyone's silver or gold or clothing. You yourselves know that
these hands of mine have supplied my own needs and the needs of my
companions. In everything I did, I showed you that by this kind of hard
work we must help the weak, remembering the words the Lord Jesus
himself said: "It is more blessed to give than to receive."

—ACTS 20:32–35

Well, we are finally there—Christmas day—the climax of our twenty-five-day odyssey to the heart of Christmas. And although at first blush it may seem an odd one, I want to ask you a question: *Do you have the Christmas spirit?* I mean, do you *really* have the Christmas spirit? Better yet, what *is* the Christmas spirit? Is it the warm and familiar feeling of being with family and friends around a soothing fire and flickering candlelight? Is it the joy of seeing anticipation in the eyes of a child? Is it the satisfaction of unwrapping a special gift? Or is the spirit of Christmas something else?

The answer is found in Christ, who for our sake came that Christmas morn two thousand years ago. Who for our sake condescended to cloak Himself in human flesh. Who emptied Himself. Who "made himself nothing, taking the very nature of a servant, being made in human likeness. And being found in appearance as a man" (Philippians 2:7–8). Who, far from grasping the prerogatives of divinity, "humbled himself" (v. 8).

That, I would argue, is the spirit of Christmas. It is not the rush we experience *when we get*—get a gift, get a feeling, get a bonus. All these are wonderful in and of themselves. The real spirit of Christmas, however, is found not in what we *get*, but in what we *give*. It is becoming ever more like our Savior in the spirit of selflessness. And not just during the Christmas season or on Christmas Day, but rather throughout the remainder of our lives.

This Christmas season, my family and I have a prayer for you just as we have a prayer for ourselves. It is that as we see images of the poor standing in soup lines on our television screens, we might see ourselves placing a piece of bread in the hands of the hungry. As we remember those in nursing homes, we might envision ourselves dispensing a hug. As we remember the widows and the orphans, we might imagine ourselves healing their hurts. Ultimately, doing so is in the service of dispensing the bread of life. "I am the bread of life," said Jesus. "He who comes to me will never go hungry, and he who believes in me will never be thirsty. . . . I am the living bread that came down from heaven. If anyone eats of this bread, he will live forever" (John 6:35, 51).

So, as you see, the spirit of Christmas is not a once-a-year experience. It is a spirit to be embraced throughout the coming year. It is the spirit of Ebenezer Scrooge who experienced a complete metamorphosis after his encounters with the *spirit of Christmas past*, the *spirit of Christmas present*, and the *spirit of Christmas yet to come*. It is the spirit I want reborn in my soul as each Christmas my family and I watch yet another rendition of *A Christmas Carol* by Charles Dickens.

So this year, as you and I wish each other a Merry Christmas and a Happy New Year, you and I know exactly what we mean! Merry Christmas, dear friend . . . and to all a Happy New Year!

READING

Then the King will say to those on his right, "Come, you who are blessed by my Father; take your inheritance, the kingdom prepared for you since the creation of the world. For I was hungry and you gave me something to eat, I was thirsty and you gave me something to drink, I was a stranger and you invited me in, I needed clothes and you clothed me, I was sick and you looked after me, I was in prison and you came to visit me."

Then the righteous will answer him, "Lord, when did we see you hungry and feed you, or thirsty and give you something to drink? When did we see you a stranger and invite you in, or needing clothes and clothe you? When did we see you sick or in prison and go to visit you?"

The King will reply, "I tell you the truth, whatever you did for one of the least of these brothers of mine, you did for me." (Matthew 25:34–40)

QUESTIONS

+ What is the spirit of Christmas?
+ What traditions might help your family more fully embrace the spirit of Christmas?

AWAY IN A MANGER

Verses 1–2 Anonymous
Verse 3 by John Thomas McFarland

Away in a manger, no crib for a bed,
The little Lord Jesus laid down His sweet head;
The stars in the sky looked down where He lay,
The little Lord Jesus, asleep on the hay.

The cattle are lowing, the Baby awakes,
But little Lord Jesus, no crying He makes.
I love Thee, Lord Jesus, look down from the sky,
And stay by my side till morning is nigh.

Be near me, Lord Jesus, I ask Thee to stay
Close by me forever and love me, I pray;
Bless all the dear children in Thy tender care,
And fit us for heaven to live with Thee there.

NOTES

1. William Lane Craig, "Did Jesus Rise from the Dead?" in Michael J. Wilkins and J. P. Moreland, eds., *Jesus Under Fire* (Grand Rapids: Zondervan Publishing House, 1995), 147-148; Paul Copan, ed., *Will the Real Jesus Please Stand Up? A Debate between William Lane Craig and John Dominic Crossan* (Grand Rapids: Baker Books, 1998), 26–27.

2. C. H. Dodd, "The Appearances of the Risen Christ: A Study in the Form Criticism of the Gospels," in *More New Testament Studies* (Manchester: University of Manchester, 1968), 128; as quoted in William Lane Craig, *Reasonable Faith* (Wheaton, IL: Crossway Books, 1994), 282.

3. Simon Greenleaf, *The Testimony of the Evangelists: The Gospels Examined by the Rules of Evidence* (Grand Rapids: Kregel Classics, 1995, originally published in 1874), 31–32.

4. "Although the original minutes of this council were destroyed, people have tried to reconstruct the list of bishops who agreed to the orthodox formula to describe the Trinity, a brief text that became famous as the Nicene Creed. This list is known from eleven medieval copies. Only three of them mention Nicholas, but one of these is considered to be among the best copies." Taken from "Saint Nicholas, Sinterklaas, Santa Claus," *Livius*, http://www.livius.org/ne-nn/nicholas/nicholas_of_myra1.html (accessed August 26, 2008).

5. "Christmas tree," *Encyclopædia Britannica*, 2008. *Encyclopædia Britannica Online*, http://www.britannica.com/EBchecked/topic/115737/Christmas-tree (accessed August 26, 2008).

6. D. A. Carson, "Matthew," in Frank E. Gaebelein, ed., *The Expositor's Bible Commentary*, vol. 8 (Grand Rapids: Regency Reference Library, 1984), 85.

7. Nicolas D. Kristof, "Believe It, or Not" *New York Times*, August 15, 2003, Opinion, http://www.nytimes.com/2003/08/15/opinion/15KRIS.html (last accessed May 10, 2009).

CHRISTIAN RESEARCH INSTITUTE

On the Internet (including 24-hour credit card ordering):
www.equip.org

By Mail:
CRI United States
P.O. Box 8500
Charlotte, NC 28271-8500

By Phone:
U.S. Toll-Free Customer Service Line (888) 7000-CRI
Fax (704) 887-8299

In Canada:
CRI Canada
56051 Airways P.O.
Calgary, Alberta T2E 8K5

Canada Toll-Free Credit Card Line (800) 665-5851
Canada Customer Service (403) 571-6363

On the Broadcast:
To contact the *Bible Answer Man* broadcast with your questions,
call toll-free in the U.S. and Canada, (888) ASK HANK (275-4265),
Monday–Friday, 5:50 p.m. to 7:00 p.m. Eastern Time. For a list of stations
airing the *Bible Answer Man* broadcast or to listen online,
log on to www.equip.org.

HANK HANEGRAAFF is president of the famed
Christian Research Institute International and host of the
Bible Answer Man broadcast (for a list of radio stations or to
listen to the broadcast online, log on to www.equip.org).
Hank is the author of many best-selling books, including
Resurrection, The Prayer of Jesus, and *The Apocalypse Code.*
Additionally, he is author of *The Complete Bible Answer
Book—Collector's Edition* and *Christianity in Crisis: 21st Century.*